Eleanor

W9-ARO-012

A GOLDEN HANDBOOK OF COLLECTIBLES

STONEWARE

REGINA STEWART
GERALDINE COSENTINO

Golden Press · New York
Western Publishing Company, Inc.
Racine, Wisconsin

Acknowledgments

The pieces photographed to illustrate this book are from the collections of: John Saveriana, Regina Stewart, and Raymond Duzey.

The authors wish to express their appreciation and acknowledge the following for their generous help in checking and researching: The American Life Foundation, Watkins Glen, New York; Will Anderson, author of *The Beer Book;* Kay Baker Antiques, Amherst, Massachusetts; Eleanor M. Gehres, Denver Public Library, Denver, Colorado; Virginia R. Hawley, The Western Reserve Historical Society, Cleveland, Ohio; The Historical Society of York County, York, Pennsylvania; Peter Lundell; Charles Marootian; R. W. Mauk; The New York Historical Society, New York, New York; Donald D. Pace, Robinson-Ransbottom Pottery Company, Roseville, Ohio; Samuel Pennington, editor of the *Maine Antique Digest;* Brandon Stewart; Edward T. Swasey; Society for the Preservation of New England Antiquities, Boston, Massachusetts; and The Warren County Library, Monmouth, Illinois.

ART DIRECTOR: Remo Cosentino
DESIGN: Elizabeth Alexander
PHOTOGRAPHY: John Garetti

Library of Congress Catalog Card Number: 76-55048

Contents

Introduction

During the past decade there has been increasing interest in the field of American salt-glazed decorated stoneware. Collectors of Americana have acquired stoneware as examples of American folk pottery, while many others have purchased pieces simply for their attractive decorative qualities.

American stoneware is an extremely hard, nonporous pottery, fired and glazed with common salt, and often decorated with cobalt blue. Its imperviousness to water and its durability made it extremely useful and popular as a basic household item from the seventeenth century through the early twentieth century. Stoneware crocks and jars were ideal for the storage, salting, and pickling of foods. Jugs and bottles were used for beer, vinegar, whiskey, water, and molasses. Although the most familiar stoneware shapes are crocks and jugs, other items made from stoneware were flasks, batter jugs, pitchers, bowls, pans, bean pots, foot warmers, mugs, inkwells, banks, poultry fountains, butter churns, spittoons, and flowerpots.

The technique of salt-glazing stoneware originated in the Rhineland during the fifteenth century. During the seventeenth and eighteenth centuries, Rhenish stoneware was made for export to England and continental Europe. It was shipped to the American colonies from England until the Revolutionary War, when native American potteries began to take over the market. Although European stoneware included ornamental as well as utilitarian pieces, American stoneware potters produced primarily utilitarian household items.

The American stoneware industry was dependent on a fine white clay not readily available in all parts of the United States. Almost all stoneware potteries, therefore, had to import the clay from vast deposits found in New Jersey and

Facing page: Delicately brushed flowers decorate this jar made by the William MacQuoid pottery of New York City.

Poultry fountains, used for watering poultry, were designed to keep dirt and baby chicks from falling into the water. The two above are coated with dark brown slip: The one on the left was made by Whitmore, Robinson & Company; the unmarked piece on the right is attributed to the Enterprise Pottery Company of Pennsylvania. Neither of the examples below has a maker's mark.

Long Island. This fact explains why many potteries were located near water. It enabled them to receive shipments of clay by boat, and aided them in distributing the finished wares.

The earliest stoneware potteries were located in New York, New Jersey, and coastal New England. Gradually the industry spread, following the waterways into the interior of New York, Pennsylvania, New England, Ohio, and the West. There were never a great many stoneware companies in the Southeastern United States.

The shapes and styles of early American stoneware were originally derived from European examples, but by the nineteenth century, typically American forms had evolved. Decorations not found on the European pieces were another uniquely American contribution. Images taken from the potter's environment provided motifs such as flowers, leaves, and birds. Ships, people, scenes, and patriotic symbols were also used, although they were less common.

During the height of stoneware manufacture, quantity was important, not quality or other esthetic considerations. The pieces were made quickly and sold cheaply. Nonetheless, this utilitarian ware exhibited a certain charm. Particularly appealing to collectors of stoneware today are the different shapes, decorations, and identifying marks.

During the last half of the nineteenth century, mass-produced tin and glass containers replaced those made of stoneware. New mechanical processes replaced the potter-craftsman. By the beginning of the twentieth century the salt-glazed stoneware industry had died out. However, due to the enormous quantity of pieces produced over the years, many of its products are still in existence. The stoneware pieces illustrated here are representative of what is available to the collector today.

This book is intended as a general introduction to the field of American stoneware. Not only the serious collector, but also those who enjoy owning only an occasional piece or two of stoneware will find it helpful to learn about the processes involved in manufacturing, decorating, and producing this handsome pottery. Therefore, we have included information about manufacturing techniques and methods of decoration, and a discussion of various stoneware shapes. A brief history of the American stoneware industry from its early days to its decline is also provided.

Throughout the nineteenth century, potters marked many pieces with their name and location. These maker's marks, when they appear, not only identify the manufacturer but are also valuable in dating the piece. A reference list of potters and potteries has been given so that individual stoneware pieces can be more accurately identified and dated. There is a bibliography for those who wish to do more reading and research. Information on purchasing and care is also provided, as are ideas on displaying your pieces.

There are many reasons for collecting stoneware. Among them are interest in American history, associations with the regions where stoneware was produced, and the attractiveness of the ware itself. Whether you own several pieces or a large collection, this guide will help you to appreciate the craftsmanship and historical background of your stoneware collection.

History

The primary stoneware producing areas in Europe developed along the Rhine Valley, where, by the fifteenth century, Rhenish potters developed the technique of salt glazing. Rhenish salt-glazed stoneware was made for export to England and other European countries during the seventeenth and eighteenth centuries. These pieces—food and wine containers, mugs, tankards, and storage jars—were dipped in a brown coating before they were salt-glazed. By the eighteenth century, Rhenish potters began exporting gray salt-glazed pieces decorated with cobalt blue, without the brown coating.

Stoneware was also manufactured in England in the seventeenth century. The English made not only utilitarian items but fine tableware and decorative pieces as well. English salt-glazed ware reached its peak at the end of the eighteenth century.

In the United States, stoneware wasn't produced on a large scale until after the Revolution. This was due in part to the abundance of imported Rhenish and English ware. Other factors delaying American manufacture were lack of knowledge of salt-glazing and other manufacturing techniques, and the need for large deposits of suitable clay.

Before the Revolutionary War, as national feeling grew in the colonies, there was some support for native industries that could manufacture the household goods that were being imported. As workmen came from England and the Rhineland, bringing with them the designs, formulas, and methods used in making pottery, a number of small, local potteries arose that catered to the needs of their communities. These early colonial potteries were located in New Jersey, New York, and Philadelphia.

The Revolutionary War stimulated native industries—and stopped the importation of goods from England. Although England tried to recapture the American market after the

Revolution, the immigration of skilled artisans and the discovery of important stoneware clay deposits aided the growth of the American pottery industry.

American stoneware, in general, was based on the Rhenish gray stoneware with blue decorations rather than the brown-glazed styles. During the late eighteenth century and the nineteenth century, American stoneware became more and more popular; by the nineteenth century a typically American utilitarian pottery had developed.

EASTERN STONEWARE

New York, New Jersey, and Pennsylvania were adjacent to the major Northeastern stoneware clay beds, with the greatest amount of this clay being found in the vicinity of Bayonne, New Jersey. There were also large deposits at Huntington, Long Island, and on Staten Island. New York became the major Eastern stoneware manufacturer and supplier, and New York-marked pots can be found all through the Eastern United States.

New York. The first potteries of New York City were located in lower Manhattan near the Hudson River, where they could easily receive shipments of clay from the New Jersey and New York clay beds by sloop or barge. One of the earliest of these potteries was built by John William Crolius. He was born in Coblenz, Germany, in 1700 and emigrated to New York in 1718. The exact date of the opening of his pottery is not known, but by 1730 it was located at the foot of Pottbaker's Hill. Crolius's descendants carried on the business at various locations in lower Manhattan until 1849.

Another early New York potter was John Remmey, born in Neuweid, Germany, in 1706. He emigrated to New York about 1731 and established his pottery near Crolius's about 1735. The Remmey pottery was operated by his descendants until about 1831. Some of the pieces made by the Remmey and Crolius potteries may be seen in the collections of museums and of those individuals and dealers interested in early Americana.

By the early nineteenth century, potters had moved north of

Left: The N. A. White & Son pottery, noted for the intensity of its cobalt blue decorations, made this jug. Right: A deep tan jug by J. Fisher pottery, Lyons, New York.

Decorated stoneware bowls are rare. A tulip motif enhances this piece, made by Cowden & Wilcox of Harrisburg, Pennsylvania.

the congested lower Manhattan area. Their factories needed more space, and the kilns had become a fire hazard in this crowded part of the city.

New York City merchants and businessmen wished to become involved in the growing trade with the new Western states and territories, but land travel was expensive, and the cost of shipping goods by land was prohibitive. With the opening of the Erie Canal in 1825, which connected the Hudson River to the Great Lakes, an inland waterway was created that cut the cost and time of shipping goods to the Midwest and helped establish New York as an important business center in the United States.

The Erie Canal shipped stoneware clay from New Jersey and Long Island to potteries which had opened in Utica, Geddes, Lyons, and Rochester. Other New York State potteries were located in Ellenville, Binghamton, Fort Edward, Poughkeepsie, Troy, Syracuse, and Albany. There was great competition among the New York potters. Companies frequently changed hands or merged with each other in order to remain in business. This kind of competition did not occur elsewhere, where local potteries produced only what was needed in the immediate vicinity. Many pieces of stoneware available today were made in these upstate New York factories.

New Jersey. Early New Jersey potters were James Morgan, a captain in the Revolutionary War, who opened a pottery about 1775 in the Cheesequake area near what is now South Amboy; Thomas Warne, who operated near the same locality, about 1778, and was joined by his son-in-law Joshua Letts in 1805; and Xerxes Price, who had a pottery from approximately 1802 to 1830 near what is now Sayreville.

Later pottery centers were located in Newark, Elizabeth, and Trenton. The Union Pottery, founded in Newark, New Jersey, in 1877, operated until 1906. Many New Jersey pieces found today were made by this company.

Pennsylvania. A major source of clay was found in the Philadelphia area, where the earliest Pennsylvania potters were established. One of the earliest known stoneware shops in

Philadelphia was operated by a French Huguenot immigrant, Anthony Duché, and his sons in the late 1720s. Another early Philadelphia potter was Henry Remmey, a brother of the New York potter John Remmey, who established a pottery in Philadelphia about 1810.

A major nineteenth-century producer of stoneware in Pennsylvania was the company of Cowden and Wilcox in Harrisburg. Most of their pieces were well decorated and marked. They operated from 1870 until 1881. Another well-known Pennsylvania potter was John Bell of Waynesboro, who operated his pottery from 1833 until his death in 1880. Pennsylvania stoneware was produced well into the twentieth century in the New Brighton area.

NEW ENGLAND STONEWARE

Massachusetts. The clays found in New England were not suitable for the production of stoneware. Clay for stoneware had to be shipped from Pennsylvania, New Jersey, or Long Island. Isaac Parker of Charlestown, Massachusetts, brought one of Anthony Duché's sons, James, from Pennsylvania to Massachusetts to help him develop a stoneware factory.

However, Parker died shortly after Duché's arrival in 1742. Parker's wife, Grace, convinced of the superiority of stoneware over other kinds of pottery for household use, continued the business. Duché's first attempts to make stoneware with New England clay failed, so he had clay shipped from Philadelphia. Transporting the clay was expensive and the business was not profitable. Nevertheless, Grace Parker did succeed in introducing to New England the stoneware which would eventually replace all other kinds of utilitarian pottery.

The first successful stoneware manufacturer in Massachusetts was William Seaver of Taunton. He started producing stoneware about 1790 with clay from New Jersey.

Connecticut. Stoneware became a major industry in Connecticut and New England through the efforts of Adam States of Greenwich, Connecticut. He opened his pottery about 1750. The clay he used came from Huntington, Long Island, and was shipped to Connecticut across the Long Island Sound. He and his family established factories throughout the state. Another major stoneware center was Norwalk. Stoneware pieces from this area were sold all along the Atlantic seaboard.

New Hampshire had only two potteries that produced stoneware. There was Martin Crafts at Nashua, who owned a pottery from 1838 to 1852, and Starkey and Howard, who operated one in Keene from 1871 to 1874.

Maine. Although there was no stoneware clay in Maine, several potteries did develop. Martin Crafts of New Hampshire established a branch of his pottery in Portland that was operated by Caleb Crafts until 1841. John T. Winslow established a pottery about 1850. His descendants still manage the Portland Stoneware Company.

Rufus Lamson and Eban Swasey began producing stoneware under the name Portland Pottery Works in 1881. Lamson left the company in 1890; however, E. Swasey and Company continued in business until the 1930s, even though Swasey himself died in 1906.

Vermont. Although it too was lacking in suitable clay, Vermont became a major nineteenth-century stoneware center. Stoneware made in Bennington and Burlington was widely distributed throughout the New England area.

Captain John Norton founded a pottery works in Bennington in 1793. He brought clay from New Jersey, and the Norton Company began making the crocks, jars, churns, and jugs that were to become famous. They were made of high-quality New Jersey clay. Many were skillfully decorated. Although Norton retired in 1823, his family operated the company until 1894. Many of the heavily decorated, marked pieces of New England stoneware available today are from Bennington.

SOUTHERN STONEWARE

Southern stoneware potteries were usually small companies that distributed their wares locally and did not sell them out-

Facing page: Highly decorated pitchers are hard to find. Further information about this one, photo 89, is on page 115.

side their immediate area. Few of these pieces were marked or decorated, and attributions are not often possible.

Two early Southern potters were William Rogers of Yorktown, Virginia, who worked during the 1730s, and Andrew Duché, who made pottery in South Carolina and then Georgia until about 1743. Stoneware was produced in North Carolina in the late 1700s. Many North Carolina potteries were in the vicinity of Steeds, an area commonly called Jugtown.

In the nineteenth century there were pottery manufacturers in Arkansas, Alabama, Kentucky, Maryland, Virginia, West Virginia, Tennessee, Georgia, and Florida. The Bird Brothers had a shop in Princeton, Arkansas, from 1843 to 1862, and there were many potteries active in Benton, Arkansas, from the late 1860s to the early 1900s.

Southern potters kept producing well into the twentieth century. The Bethune Pottery of South Carolina, which was founded about 1870, is still in existence. Peter Perrine started a pottery in Baltimore, Maryland, in 1793, and it was continued by his descendants until 1938.

MIDWESTERN STONEWARE

The pottery industry began moving west by the middle of the nineteenth century. The Midwest had suitable clay and good transportation, which made it possible to manufacture and distribute stoneware inexpensively.

Much of the late stoneware found today was made in the pottery centers of Ohio, Illinois, and Minnesota about 1880 to 1920. Ohio became an important manufacturing center with factories in East Liverpool, Springfield, Cleveland, Akron (called Stoneware City), Zanesville, and Columbus. In 1877 the Red Wing Stoneware Company was founded in Red Wing, Minnesota, becoming one of the leading stoneware makers by incorporating with their local competition. Their pieces can be found all over the United States. They used mass-production methods and their pieces had minimal decoration. They produced stoneware until the 1940s, finally going out of busi-

Facing page: Hand-dated pieces are rarities. A Spencerian swirl underlines the date on this F. B. Norton & Company jug.

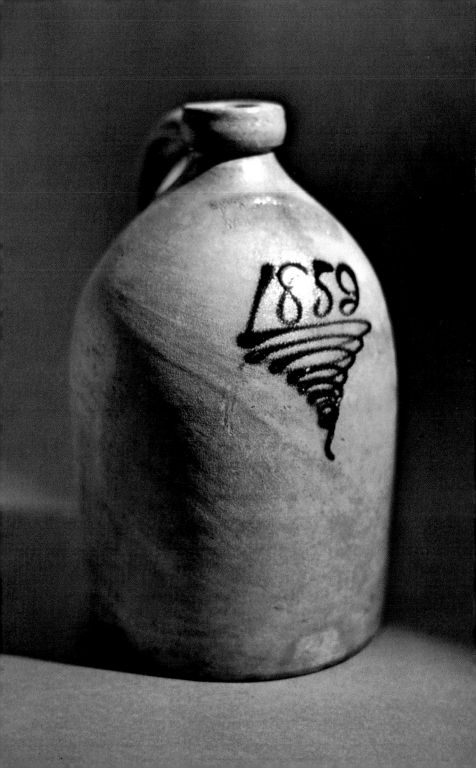

ness in 1967. Stoneware was also produced in Indiana, Iowa, Wisconsin, Kansas, and Nebraska.

SOUTHWESTERN AND WESTERN STONEWARE

Texas. Salt-glazed stoneware was made in Texas from before the Civil War until the 1920s. One of the earliest potteries was opened by Hirum Wilson, an ex-slave, about 1870. Many of the Texas potters marked their stoneware, and there is quite a bit of marked Texas stoneware available.

California had stoneware potteries in East Oakland, Los Angeles, Michigan Bar, and Sacramento. Marked pieces of stoneware can be found from J. A. Bauer & Company of Los Angeles, and from the Los Angeles Stoneware Company.

Oregon. The first pottery in Oregon was made by Barnet Ramsey, near Springfield, about 1853. His company remained active in various locations until 1868. The Pacific Pottery Company of Portland was opened about 1892 and produced stoneware until the 1950s. There were also stoneware makers in Alban, Buena Vista, and Halsey.

LATE STONEWARE

Stoneware filled a need in the eighteenth and nineteenth centuries. No other material could fulfill so many purposes. It was good for storing, pickling, and preserving foods. Its sturdiness, its imperviousness to moisture, and its ability not to add odors or tastes to foods made it a necessity in early homes.

With the coming of new techniques in home canning, mechanical refrigeration, and the availability of inexpensive glass jars and bottles and tin storage containers, the need for stoneware diminished. By the mid 1800s small companies could no longer stay in business, and even the large factories had to use mass-production molding and casting methods in order to compete in price with each other. By the beginning of the twentieth century, the attractive salt-glazed stoneware decorated with cobalt blue was no longer being produced. In its place was a mechanically made, undecorated replica of the earlier handmade products.

Manufacture

Pottery is classified according to its hardness and the characteristics and composition of the clay from which it is formed. The hardness of the finished or fired pottery is determined by the presence and amounts of the essential components silica and kaolin in the clay from which the pottery is made. Stoneware clay produced a heavy, hard pottery that is resistant to odors and tastes and is vitreous—even unglazed it will not absorb water.

Almost all stoneware potteries imported their clays. When the clay arrived it was usually dry and often mixed with rocks, pebbles, and sand. A machine called a pug mill was used to break up the hardened, dry clay and mix it with water to make it pliable. The pug mill was a cylindrical tank with metal spikes or blades projecting from the inner wall. A vertical center shaft with projecting spikes or blades was turned by a horse or some other source of power, crushing the clay and mixing it with water. It was then worked through a screen to remove any lumps or stones. Some manufacturers added local clays to the imported clays. This often resulted in poor quality stoneware, porous and breakable. After the clay was cleaned it was wedged, a kneading process that insured uniform moisture.

In small potteries, the potters could do all the work; in large potteries, the work was divided. One man could not meet the needs of a large company, and so specialization came about as an economic necessity. There would be throwers, and finishers who completed the work. There might be an assistant who did nothing but apply handles and spouts, and others who decorated the ware. There were even apprentices who readied the clay on the wheel, a table attached to a revolving stand.

The master potter or thrower took a predetermined amount of clay, depending on what he was going to make, and threw it on the wheel. He centered the lump of clay, and turning the wheel base with his feet, he shaped the crock or jug using his thumbs, his fingers, and the palms of his hands. The potter had to be a quick worker and a skilled craftsman. Using few tools, he relied on his judgement and experience to make the pieces uniform. He often made several hundred items a day. His tools were simple wood or ceramic scrapers and ribs, which he used to smooth and shape the pieces as they turned on the wheel. A sponge was used to give the pieces a smooth finish. Handles, spouts, and surface decorations were applied separately. They were made of clay and formed by hand or in molds. The clay additions were applied by pressing them into place with the thumbs. Then the pot was cut from the wheel with a piece of wire. The name of the pottery might be impressed on the finished piece.

The stoneware was dried from one to three days out in the open or in a special drying oven. Called greenware at this stage, the dried, unglazed pots were then coated on the inside with a brownish or blackish clay known as Albany slip. (Albany slip came from the banks of the Hudson River near Albany, and was used to coat or seal the inside of pieces made after 1800.) Next, the outside might be decorated, and then the ware was ready to be fired.

The firing was done in a kiln, a large heavy-walled brick-lined oven that was heated by means of wood fires. The pottery was stacked in the kilns in layers, which were filled as full as possible. Sometimes the pieces on the bottom layer were dented or buckled as a result of the weight piled on them. The pottery rested on setting tiles and were separated by pieces of raw clay. The temperature of the kiln was raised to the maximum slowly, which removed any moisture left in the ware and helped to prevent cracking.

Once the kiln was heated to the temperature for stoneware, 2200 or 2300 degrees Fahrenheit, the salt glazing was begun. Common salt was shoveled down into the kiln, which was opened and closed from the top. The salt would vaporize in the high temperature, covering every exposed surface. As the sodium in the salt combined with the silica in the clay, a hard glaze was formed on the body of the pottery. After salt glazing, the fires were kept at maximum for a few days and then slowly reduced. The kiln was cooled as carefully as it had been heated. The whole process took from six to eight days.

Kiln accidents were common. Stacks of pots collapsed, or the pieces at the bottom buckled. Glazes were unevenly applied and pieces were unevenly fired. Occasionally too much local clay had been added to the stoneware clay and the entire contents of the kiln were ruined. Almost every piece of stoneware had some imperfection, burn, or malformation.

COLOR

Most clays contained impurities, such as iron oxides and organic matter, that gave color to the stoneware. The color varied from gray to cream, buff, tan, pink, red, and brown. The stoneware clay from Pennsylvania, New Jersey, and New York created various gray shades. When local clays were mixed with the stoneware clay, various buffs, creams, pinks, tans, and grays could be found in one piece.

There was no effort made to control the color of early stoneware. Uniform color was only produced when the exterior of a piece was glazed entirely with white, cream, or brown slip (liquid clay). By the late 1800s and early 1900s, it became popular to dip the upper portion of a piece in brown slip and coat the lower part with a white or cream-colored slip.

TEXTURE

The texture of stoneware was created by the composition of the clay, the finish given the surface of the piece, and the results of salt glazing. These textures varied from piece to piece. Coarse clay often gave a pebbly, grainy surface. If the body of the stoneware wasn't smoothed, there might be ridges left by the potter's hands as he shaped the piece. Depending on the amount of salt used and the effects of the firing, the salt left textures from shiny to dull, and from smooth to the orange-peel-like surface that is typical of most stoneware.

Decorating Techniques

Several techniques were used in decorating stoneware: incising, impressing, glazing with a slip cup or brush, and stenciling. These decorations were used to give variety, color, and interest to stoneware, whose basic shapes were similar due to their functional rather than ornamental purpose.

The shapes of the stoneware and the type of decorative techniques used are helpful in approximating the date of a piece. Many of the eighteenth-century and early nineteenth-century forms were ovoid. These pieces had small bases from which the body flared out and then curved back at the shoulder. Generally, the smaller the base in proportion to the body, the earlier the piece. These early forms, which were attractive in themselves, were usually not heavily decorated. The curved forms made elaborate decoration difficult, and designs were often confined to the broader upper portion of the ware. In-

Noah White founded a number of potteries in New York State that operated successfully for about seventy years. The crock on the left was made in Utica sometime between 1865 and 1877; the piece on the right, in Binghamton between 1882 and 1888.

cising and impressing, with either a coggle wheel or a stamp, were the decorating techniques used on late eighteenth-century and early nineteenth-century pieces.

As the nineteenth century progressed, more easily produced shapes became popular. The bases widened and the sides became straighter. By the mid-nineteenth century, most stoneware companies produced straight-sided ware. This later shape lent itself to more elaborate decorations using glazing and, later, stenciling.

DECORATORS

In early and small potteries it was usually the potter who decorated his own ware. As business expanded, specialization became necessary and people were hired specifically as decorators. Most decorators learned their skills informally since there was little in the way of written instructions. The decorators were often itinerant workers who traveled from pottery to pottery as their services were needed. This resulted in similarly decorated pieces from different potteries.

INCISING

Incising was the most time-consuming method of decorating. It was a laborious procedure done by freehand sketching with either a plain wooden-handled instrument with a sharp blade or a thin iron rod, which cut into the still soft clay. The designs produced this way were usually simple and often small in relation to the size of the stoneware. Flowers, leaves, and birds, either real or imaginary, were popular motifs. Ships, fish, and figures were uncommon. Patriotic designs, inspired by the War of 1812, resulted in highly decorated incised symbols of eagles (the most popular), the American flag, national figures, and naval scenes. Most of this type of decoration was not made in great quantity and these pieces are relatively rare. Incised decorations were often highlighted with cobalt blue.

IMPRESSING

Impressing with either a coggle wheel or a stamp was a more mechanical process than incising.

Coggling. The coggle was a small wheel with a decorative motif in relief mounted on a wooden handle. It was rotated against the piece as the piece was turned on the potter's wheel. This created decorations of lines, bands, or repeated motifs, which were often highlighted with cobalt blue. These circumferential designs were usually placed around the top rim of the ware.

Stamping. A stamp made of fired clay or carved wood with a design in relief was pressed into the still soft pot. These stamped pieces resembled the hand-incised ones, but required less time and skill. Sometimes they were used in combination with hand incising to produce more complex designs than either method could alone. Stamped designs were often highlighted with cobalt blue by either dipping the stamp into blue glaze before each impression, or by brushing the glaze on over the finished design. One of the most popular stamp designs was the swag and tassel motif. A stamp of wood, fired clay, or printer's type was used for impressing the maker's mark.

As the nineteenth century progressed, quantity sales became the goal. Since the pottery was a small manufacturing business rather than a craft shop, a design had to be done rapidly to be economical. This led to the use of faster decorating techniques, such as brush and slip-cup glazing, which replaced the incised and stamped designs of the early 1800s.

GLAZING

The most common form of decoration was glazing with cobalt, a dark blue metallic oxide that fired to a glasslike finish. This was the best oxide for use on stoneware since it was stable when fired—that is, the color did not change or break down—and it blended well with the grays and tans of stoneware. Cobalt was a very strong coloring agent and little was needed to produce the glaze, which made it economical. To apply the cobalt oxide to the ware, it was first mixed with silica and gum arabic, which dissolved in water to make a thick paste or liquid. It was then painted on the dried greenware with either a brush or a slip cup.

Manganese was also used for glazing. It fired to a dark brown or black, but was never as popular as cobalt blue.

Brushwork. A stiff brush was used to paint motifs on the stoneware in short, spontaneous strokes. Brushwork enabled the decorator to create more lively, realistic designs. It replaced incised and impressed decorations in the 1820s.

The slip cup. The slip cup, which made very elaborate decoration possible, came into use in the mid-1800s. The cup was a small, hand-held pottery container with an opening for filling at the top and another opening fitted with a quill on the front. As the cup was tilted, the glaze flowed through the quill onto the pot. Thickness of line was controlled by manipulating the cup. This technique allowed the decorator to make long, uninterrupted lines. Combined with short, wide brushstrokes, some of the most complex designs were created.

The slip cup was also used to create calligraphic designs. These were the Spencerian script motifs that resembled handwriting exercises. They were influenced by the highly ornamental formal handwriting of the eighteenth and nineteenth centuries.

Most decorations created with the slip cup were placed on the front of the ware. Among the standard designs were florals, leaves, birds, and Spencerian motifs. More unusual decorations were scenes and figures. Popular scenes included sailing ships; landscapes, some depicting houses or other buildings; and animals in forest or mountain settings. Figures tended to be humorous and were usually made for individual purchasers rather than for general sales. Most of the decorated stoneware found today was made during this period.

STENCILING

After the Civil War stencils became popular. They reduced the time spent on decoration. Stencils were most popular in Pennsylvania and West Virginia. The stenciled designs were made by tracing with glaze through a stencil held against the side of the stoneware. Stencils usually included the potter's name and location, a decorative design, or objects such as stars, eagles, fruit, or flowers. Bands or wavy lines were often brushed above and/or below the stenciled design to offset its severity.

Stencils were also used on commercial pieces to mark the name and location of the wholesale purchaser.

MAKER'S MARKS

In pottery, the word *mark* refers to a name, monogram, initial, or symbol which is impressed, painted, embossed, scratched, stenciled, or stamped on an individual piece. The mark usually indicates the maker, and helps to establish the date of production. The custom of marking stoneware with the potter's name and location was used from about 1800 through the 1890s. Changes in ownership, mergers, the addition or departure of a partner, son, or relative often resulted in a variety of marks being used during a pottery's operation.

The marks were impressed in still soft clay with a printer's lead-type stamp set in a wooden handle. Potters in Pennsylvania, Virginia, and West Virginia used stencils to mark their ware during the second half of the nineteenth century. Late nineteenth-century and early twentieth-century makers used rubber stamps to imprint their mark. Often the printer's stamp was dipped in cobalt blue glaze, or the impressed mark was brushed with cobalt to highlight the potter's name. Because of the rounded shapes of the stoneware, the first and last letters of these marks are sometimes missing or not clearly impressed.

CAPACITY MARKS

A number representing the capacity of the piece was often either brushed or impressed near the maker's mark.

WHOLESALE PURCHASER'S MARKS

Occasionally the mark is not the potter's but that of the wholesale purchaser. As stoneware was replaced with more efficient materials for home use, potters limited their production to commercial containers for use by grocers, hardware stores, and liquor dealers. Butter was packed in stoneware crocks. Jugs were used for alcoholic beverages, vinegar, molasses, soda flavorings, turpentine, varnish, linseed oil, and glue. Although these pieces were not decorated, it was common practice to write the name and location of the dealer on the ware in cobalt blue script. Stencils and rubber stamps were also used to print the information on the stoneware, in either cobalt blue or manganese black glaze.

DATING

Over the years a great deal of research has been done in city directories, land deeds, and other business records to establish the dates these marks represent. Wholesale purchaser's marks can be approximately dated by checking city directories for the years that the purchaser was at a given address or location.

Unfortunately, since not all pieces are marked, attributing a date or manufacturer to an unmarked piece is difficult. In most cases there are no definite shapes or decorations that can be positively identified as being used by a particular potter.

Jugs

The jug was a round, single-handled container made to hold liquids. The mouth was small and sealed with a cork or a whittled wooden plug. Some larger jugs had two handles, which made them easier to lift. Others, made with pouring spouts, were used as containers for thick liquids such as molasses or syrup.

There were two basic jug shapes, ovoid and cylindrical. The ovoid shape was an early form in which the middle of the jug was wider than its base or top. A variation of the ovoid was the bell shape, in which the lower portion of the body was wider than its base or top. The cylindrical shape had either rounded shoulders that tapered into the neck or a ridge at the shoulder, with either a cone or funnel forming the top. These latter were called shoulder jugs.

Jugs were made in sizes from one-eighth gallon to six gallons. Most jugs found today have from a half-gallon to a five-gallon capacity.

PHOTO 1
Height: 14 inches
Marked: S. Hart/Fulton

This very attractively shaped slightly ovoid jug has an elaborate design of two birds in cobalt blue.

James and Samuel Hart operated a pottery in Oswego Falls, New York, from 1832 until 1840. (The name Oswego Falls was changed to Fulton in the 1830s.) James Hart sold his share of the pottery and moved to Sherburne, where he opened his own pottery in 1841. The maker's mark on this jug represents the period from 1840 to 1876, when Samuel Hart was sole owner.

PHOTO 1

PHOTO 2

Left
Height: 13½ inches
Marked: N. Clark & Co./Lyons

A large number "2" capacity mark was brushed on the upper portion of this extremely ovoid jug.

The Athens, New York, potter Nathan Clark established a branch of his pottery in Lyons, New York, in 1822 when the Erie Canal was opened in that area. This pottery was in operation until 1852.

Right
Height: 12 inches
Marked: J. F. Brayton & Co./Utica

A cobalt blue script-written number "2" capacity mark with a leaf design above it was brushed on the upper portion of this extremely ovoid jug.

The J. F. Brayton and Company mark represents the 1833 to c. 1837 period in the operation of this Utica, New York, pottery.

PHOTO 3

Height: 14 inches
No Maker's Mark

A cobalt blue floral motif decorates this ovoid jug.

Impressed on the jug is the name of a Poughkeepsie, New York, storekeeper: "E. Trivett, Pokeepsie, Drugs, Medicines, Paints, Oils, Glass, and Dystuffs."

PHOTO 4

Height: 18½ inches
No Maker's Mark

This Spencerian script motif is a combination of the number "5" capacity mark and a bumblebee design. Similarly decorated pieces have been attributed to a pottery in Penn Township, Indiana.

PHOTO 2

PHOTO 3

PHOTO 4

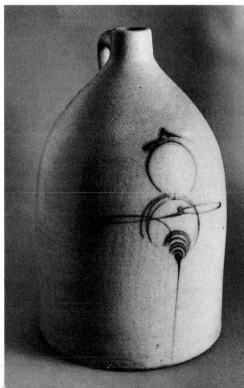

PHOTO 5

Height: 10 inches
Marked: Goodwin/&/Webster

The handle of this ovoid jug has a band of cobalt blue.

Horace Goodwin and Mack C. Webster operated their pottery in Hartford, Connecticut, c. 1810 to 1840.

PHOTO 6

Left
Height: 12 inches
Marked: Whites, Utica

The Spencerian script motif that decorates this jug is called the pine tree. It is one of a variety of Spencerian script motifs that were used on pieces from this pottery.

Noah White established his pottery in Utica, New York, in 1838. Succeeding generations ran it until 1909. The maker's mark on this jug was used from 1865 to 1877.

Right
Height: 11½ inches
Marked: Whites, Utica

The cobalt blue floral design is a simplified version of an orchid motif frequently used by the pottery that made this jug.

Noah White established his pottery in Utica, New York, in 1838. Succeeding generations ran it until 1909. The maker's mark on this jug was used from 1865 to 1877.

PHOTO 7

Height: 18½ inches
Marked: Wm. E. Warner/West Troy

This exceptional six-gallon jug has a double handle and a cobalt blue brushed tulip decoration.

William E. Warner operated a pottery in West Troy, New York, from 1829 to 1852.

PHOTO 5

PHOTO 6

PHOTO 9 ►

PHOTO 7

PHOTO 8

PHOTO 8

Height: 13 inches
Marked: N. Clark Jr./Athens, N.Y.

A cobalt blue floral motif decorates this jug, which was made with a pouring spout.

Nathan Clark, Sr., established a pottery in Athens, New York, in 1805. It was in operation until 1892 and was one of the leading New York State potteries. Clark expanded his business and established branches in Lyons, Rochester, and Mount Morris. His son Nathan Clark, Jr., operated the Athens pottery from 1843 to 1891, and it is the son's mark that is impressed in a circle on the jug.

PHOTO 9

Height: 13½ inches
Marked: N. A. White & Son/Utica, N.Y.

An elaborate floral motif with heavily brushed areas of cobalt blue decorates this jug.

Noah White established his pottery in Utica, New York, in 1838. Succeeding generations ran it until 1909. The maker's mark shown here was used during the years 1882 to 1886. Pieces having this mark are noted for the intensity of their cobalt blue decoration.

This handsome jug is illustrated in color on page 11.

PHOTO 10

Height: 10 inches
Marked: Wm. E. Warner/West Troy

The heavy cobalt blue floral decoration is combined with Spencerian flourishes, which may be initials.

William E. Warner operated his pottery in West Troy, New York, from 1829 to 1852.

PHOTO 10

PHOTO 11

PHOTO 12

PHOTO 11

Left
Height: 13 inches
Marked: J. & E. Norton/Bennington, Vt.

The extremely decorative cobalt blue flower motif suggests a rose. Several different versions of this motif, including an elaborate design of a rose surrounded by leaves in a wicker basket, were produced during the 1850s.

The J. and E. Norton mark represents the 1850 to 1859 period in the operation of the Bennington potteries.

Right
Height: 11 inches
Marked: New York/Stoneware Co./Fort Edward, N.Y.

This cobalt blue leaf design is a typical motif used by New York State decorators.

The Fort Edward area of New York State produced a great deal of stoneware during the second half of the nineteenth century. This maker's mark represents the company of George Satterlee and Michael Morey. It operated from 1861 to 1885.

PHOTO 12

Left
Height: 14½ inches
Marked: L. W. Fenton/St. Johnsbury, Vt.

A stylized feather design in cobalt blue decorates this jug.

Richard Webber Fenton established a pottery in St. Johnsbury, Vermont, in 1808. Later, his son Leander took over the business. The pottery was closed after a fire in 1859.

Right
Height: 14 inches
Marked: J. Burger Jr./Rochester, N.Y.

A Spencerian motif done in cobalt blue decorates this jug.

John Burger, Jr., joined his father's pottery in 1861. He took full control of the business in 1878 and continued to operate the pottery until 1890.

PHOTO 13
Height: 14 inches
No Maker's Mark

A bird perched on a branch, in cobalt blue, decorates this jug made for the wholesale purchaser whose name and address is impressed on the jug: "J. Keerman & Co., Importers & Wholesalers, Liquor Dealers, 22 Dean St., Albany."

PHOTO 14
Height: 11 inches
Marked: Whites, Utica

The cobalt blue parrot that decorates this jug is reminiscent of Oriental ink drawings in the quality of the line.

Noah White established his pottery in Utica, New York, in 1838. Succeeding generations ran it until 1909. The maker's mark on this jug was used from 1865 to 1877.

PHOTO 15
Height: 14 inches
Marked: J. M. Pruden/Elizabeth, N.J.

A cobalt blue nonrepresentational design is shown on this jug and can be found on many of the pieces by this maker.

John M. Pruden operated his pottery in Elizabeth, New Jersey, from 1816 to 1879.

PHOTO 16
Height: 10½ inches
Marked: E & L. P. Norton/Bennington, Vt.

This simple, brushed motif, in cobalt blue, is one of the leaf designs associated with Bennington wares.

The mark of Edward and Luman Preston Norton represents the 1861 to 1881 period in the operation of the Bennington potteries.

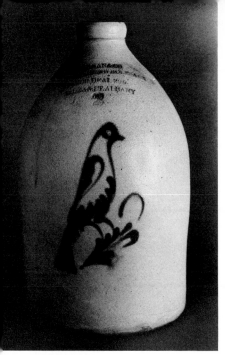

PHOTO 13

PHOTO 14

PHOTO 15

PHOTO 16

PHOTO 17
Height: 9 inches
No Maker's Mark

Embossed on the funnel-shaped shoulder of this jug is the identification of the wholesale purchaser: "Strong, Cobb & Co., Wholesale, Druggist, Cleveland." Samuel M. Strong established the business in 1833. The company manufactured medicines and imported wines and liquers. The company was listed in the Cleveland City Directories until 1972, when it became part of another corporation.

PHOTO 18
Height: 14½ inches
Marked: F. T. Wright & Son / Stoneware / Taunton, Mass.

The cobalt blue decoration on this piece shows a tiger circled by two rings. The entire design was applied with a stencil.

Franklin T. Wright operated his pottery in Taunton, Massachusetts, from 1855 to 1868. This mark was first used when his son joined the company in the 1860s.

PHOTO 19
Left
Height: 9¾ inches
No Maker's Mark

This shoulder jug was made for a wholesale purchaser. The funnel-shaped top is coated with Albany slip. Stenciled on it in cobalt blue are the words "Bauer Bros., 178 Main Ave., Passaic, N.J." Mark and Moe Bauer were wholesale liquor dealers at the listed address from 1906 to 1918.

Right
Height: 10 inches
No Maker's Mark

Stenciled on the jug in cobalt blue are the name of the wholesale purchaser, his product, and his location: "Smiley, Mineral Springs Water, E. C. Little & Sons, Haverville, Mass."

PHOTO 17

PHOTO 18

PHOTO 19

PHOTO 20

Height: 11½ inches
Marked: F. B. Norton & Co./Worcester, Mass.

The year "1859," written in cobalt blue with a typical Spencerian motif below, decorates this jug.

Franklin Blackmer Norton was the grandson of the founder of the Bennington, Vermont, potteries. An experienced potter, he set up his own shop with Frederick Hancock in Worcester, Massachusetts, in 1858. Hancock left the company in 1865. Norton was joined by his sons in the late 1860s and operated the company until 1885.

See page 17 for a color illustration of this jug.

PHOTO 21

Height: 13½ inches
Marked: J. Fisher/Lyons, N.Y.

This jug was made for the wholesale purchaser whose name and address appears in cobalt blue: "P. F. Rauber & Bro., Rochester, New York."

Jacob Fisher became sole proprietor of the Lyons Stoneware Works c. 1882. He operated the pottery until 1902, when he retired. A new owner ran the pottery until 1904.

A color photograph of this jug appears on page 11.

PHOTO 22

Height: 12 inches
No Maker's Mark

This two-gallon jug was coated with a dark brown glaze. The wholesale purchaser's name and address was scratched into the brown glaze before firing, which exposed the light-colored clay body. The purchaser was "E. L. Anderson Distilling Co., Newport, Ky."

PHOTO 20

PHOTO 21

PHOTO 22

PHOTO 23

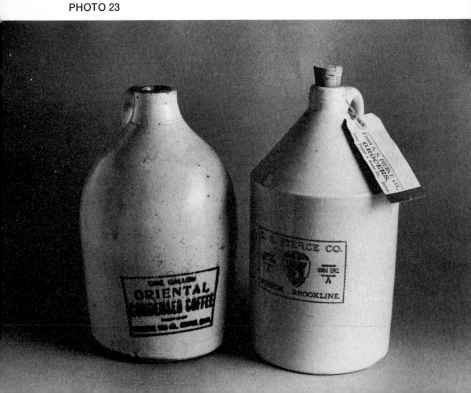

PHOTO 23

Left
Height: 11 inches
No Maker's Mark

The wholesale purchaser's name, product, and location are imprinted in cobalt blue on this jug: "One Gallon, Oriental, Condensed Coffee, Oriental Tea Co., Boston, Mass." The Oriental Tea Company was established c. 1868 and was located at 85, 87, 89 Court Street, Somerville, Massachusetts. About 1918 the company name was changed to The Oriental Tea and Coffee Company.

Right
Height: 11½ inches
Marked: R. C. P. Co./Akron, O.

This jug was made for the famous Boston grocer Silas S. Pierce. On the jug is imprinted in cobalt blue "S. S. Pierce Co.," their coat of arms, and their location, "Boston, Brookline." To the left of the coat of arms is "Est. 1831"; to the right is "1894 Inc." There is a paper address label attached to the jug which reads "From S. S. Pierce Co., Grocers, Corner Tremont & Beacon Sts., Boston." On the back of the label is "E. S. Wheeler, 1/2 Gal P.R. Molasses, 1 Gal Jug." S. S. Pierce was located at the Tremont and Beacon Streets address from 1895 to 1949.

Impressed on the base of the jug is the mark of the Robinson Clay Product Company, of Akron, Ohio. It was founded in 1856 by Thomas Robinson, his brother-in-law Richard Whitmore, and Thomas Johnson. Originally called Johnson, Whitmore & Company, the name was changed to Whitmore, Robinson & Company when they incorporated in 1862. In 1900 a new partnership was called Robinson, Merrill Pottery Company; it only lasted until 1902, when the company became the Robinson Clay Product Company (R.C.P. Co.). In 1922 Robinson merged with the Ransbottom Brothers Pottery Company, becoming the Robinson-Ransbottom Pottery Company.

PHOTO 24
Height: 13½ inches
No Maker's Mark

Impressed at the neck and repeated on the body in cobalt blue script is the name and address of the jug's wholesale purchaser: "P. Arnault, 192 Prince St., New York." Pierre Arnault was a wholesale liquor dealer and the proprietor of the Lafayette Club Whiskies. His business was located at this address from 1887 to 1890.

PHOTO 25
Height: 13¾ inches
No Maker's Mark

The wholesale purchaser's name and address is written on this jug in cobalt blue decorative script letters: "J. L. Raymond, 70 Cross St., Paterson, N.J." John L. Raymond, a "wholesale dealer in rectified and imported wines and liquors," was listed at 66, 68, 70 Cross Street, Paterson, New Jersey, from 1871 to 1895.

PHOTO 26
Left
Height: 10½ inches
No Maker's Mark

This shoulder jug was made for a wholesale purchaser. Written in cobalt blue is his name, with the message "When empty return to, A. L. Sachtleben, Hackensack, N.J."

Right
Height: 10 inches
No Maker's Mark

The funnel-shaped shoulder of this jug is coated with a dark brown glaze. The jug was made for a New Jersey brewer. Written in cobalt blue script is "Phillipsburg Brewing Co., Phillipsburg, N.J."

PHOTO 24

PHOTO 25

PHOTO 26

PHOTO 27

Height: 12 inches
No Maker's Mark

Written in heavy cobalt blue script is the name and location of the wholesale purchaser: "E. Ryan, Successor to J.R.A. Power, Paterson, N.J." Edward Ryan was a liquor dealer in Paterson, New Jersey, from 1904 to 1919.

PHOTO 28

Left
Height: 11½ inches
No Maker's Mark

The jug's wholesale purchaser was "Steinhardt Bros., & leo., 121 Hudson St., N.Y.," whose name and address appears in cobalt blue script. The Steinhardt brothers operated liquor stores in various locations in Manhattan and Brooklyn. The Hudson Street address is listed in the New York City Directories from 1893 to 1898.

Center
Height: 13½ inches
No Maker's Mark

The wholesale purchaser, "M. H. Haussling, N.J.R.R. Ave., Newark, N.J.," had his name and address written in cobalt blue script on this jug. Martin H. Haussling first appeared in the Newark City Directories in 1888 as a liquor dealer. His address was 134-138 New Jersey Railroad Avenue. The last listing for M. H. Haussling was in 1918.

Right
Height: 8½ inches
No Maker's Mark

Written in cobalt blue script is the name and address of the wholesale purchaser for whom this jug was made: "Louis Heymann, 1255 Broadway, Brooklyn."

PHOTO 27

PHOTO 29

Left
Height: 8 inches
No Maker's Mark

Scratched into the dark brown glaze is "W. P. McKough, Amsterdam, N.Y.," the wholesale purchaser of the jug.

Right
Height: 7 inches
No Maker's Mark

This jug was made for a wholesale purchaser. Scratched into the dark-brown glaze is "For pure fine Whiskey, have this Jug filled at, McGrath and Bottom's, Shelbyville, Ky."

PHOTO 30

Left
Height: 9 inches
Marked: R. C. P. Co./Akron, O.

Imprinted on this shoulder jug is "M. Salzman Co., Purity Above All," the name and motto of the wholesale purchaser who used the jug to hold whiskey. The funnel-shaped shoulder is coated with a dark brown slip.

Impressed on the base is the mark of the Robinson Clay Product Company of Akron, Ohio.

Center
Height: 11 inches
No Maker's Mark

This shoulder jug was made for Ernest Petrucci. Imprinted on the jug are Petrucci's trademark and the word "Wines." These are encircled by his name and address. Below this is printed "This Jug Is Loaned Not Sold." Mr. Petrucci, a merchant, was first listed at 488 9th Avenue, New York, in the 1901 New York City Directory.

Right
Height: 9 inches
Marked: R. C. P. Co./Akron, O.

The grocer and wine dealer Louis Jorio purchased this shoul-

PHOTO 28

PHOTO 29

PHOTO 30

PHOTO 31

der jug. Imprinted on it is "L. Jorio, Wines, 211 E. 121st St., New York." The funnel-shaped shoulder is coated with a dark brown glaze. Mr. Jorio was first listed in the New York City Directories at this address in 1895.

The mark impressed on the base was that used by the Robinson Clay Product Company of Akron, Ohio.

PHOTO 31

Left
Height: 9¼ inches
No Maker's Mark

This jug has a wire bail handle rather than one made of applied clay. Imprinted in black is the name and location of the wholesale purchaser: "The Casper Co., Inc., Roanoke, Va., Lowest Priced Whiskey House, Send for Confidential List, Our Plant Covers 14 Acres."

Right
Height: 10 inches
No Maker's Mark

The upper third of this jug made for a wholesale purchaser is coated with a dark brown glaze. The jug is imprinted in black, "Steuben County, Wine Co., 240 & 248 Madison Street, Chicago."

PHOTO 32

Left
Marked: (imprinted crown mark)

Imprinted on this shoulder jug is the wholesale purchaser's message: "P. H. Donohoe & Co., Wines and Liquors, 40 Church Street, Lowell, Mass." The funnel-shaped shoulder is coated with a dark brown slip.

The imprinted crown mark represents the Ransbottom Brothers Pottery Company, which was founded in 1900 in Roseville, Ohio. In 1922 they merged with the Robinson Clay

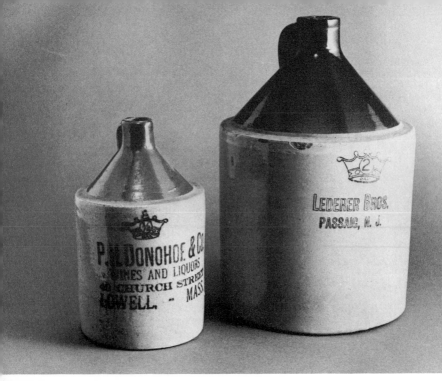

PHOTO 32

PHOTO 33

Product Company of Akron, Ohio, becoming the Robinson-Ransbottom Pottery Company.

Right
Height: 13 inches
Marked: (imprinted crown mark)

This jug was made for a wholesale purchaser: "Lederer Bros., Passaic, N.J." Albert and Rudolph Lederer were first listed in the Passaic City Directories in 1899. They were dealers in liquor, wine, malt hops, and soft drinks.

The Robinson-Ransbottom Pottery Company of Roseville, Ohio, made this jug. They are still in operation in Roseville.

PHOTO 33
Height: 11½ inches, 11½ inches, 9 inches
No Maker's Mark

All three jugs are imprinted "R. H. Macy & Co." These jugs were made for the wine and liquor department of R. H. Macy and Company of New York City. This famous department store was founded by Rowland Hussey Macy in 1858. His first store was a fancy dry goods shop at 204-206 Sixth Avenue near 14th Street. The Straus family became his partners in 1888, and by 1896 they owned the entire company. The "& Co." was first used with the Macy name in 1872.

Crocks

The crock was a round, wide-mouthed container with handles, used for storing staples and for pickling and preserving. The handles were originally round and freestanding. By the early nineteenth century most of the handles were flat, arched ridges that adhered completely to the sides of the crock.

There were two basic crock shapes, ovoid and cylindrical. The earlier ovoid shapes were wider in the middle than at the base and had a low, slightly flaring collar and rim. This curved form became less and less distinctive, and by the middle of the nineteenth century most crocks were made in a straight-sided cylindrical form. After the mid-1800s, many of the crocks came with fitted covers.

Most crocks held from one to ten gallons, although sizes up to fifty gallons are known to have been made.

PHOTO 34
Height: 13 inches
Marked: Clark & Fox / Athens

This early ovoid crock has a low, slightly flaring collar. A brushed decoration in cobalt blue is on the upper portion.

Nathan Clark and Ethan S. Fox operated their pottery in Athens, New York, from 1829 to 1838.

PHOTO 35
Height: 13 inches
Marked: M. Woodruff & Co. / Cortland

A cobalt blue flower and leaf design decorates this five-gallon ovoid crock with a slightly flared collar.

It was made by the Madison Woodruff pottery, which was in production in Cortland, New York, from 1849 to c. 1885.

PHOTO 34

PHOTO 35

PHOTO 36

PHOTO 37

PHOTO 36

Height: 11 inches
Marked: J. Hart & Son/Sherburne

The number "3" capacity mark, with three lines below it, was brushed on the upper portion of this crock. Its rather lopsided shape indicates that it was damaged in the kiln.

The maker's mark represents the years between 1841 and 1850 in the operation of the Hart pottery in Sherburne, New York.

PHOTO 37

Left
Height: 10 inches
Marked: F. H. Cowden/Harrisburg

This slightly tapered crock has a decorative geometric motif stenciled on in cobalt blue. Stenciling was a popular decorating technique of the Pennsylvania potters.

The Cowden pottery of Harrisburg, Pennsylvania, was established c. 1861. John W. Cowden formed a partnership with Isaac J. Wilcox in 1870. The company was known as Cowden & Wilcox until 1881, when Cowden's son Frederick Hatton Cowden became sole owner. He operated the pottery until 1888. Pieces made during this period were marked "F.H. Cowden, Harrisburg." In 1888 his son, John W. Cowden, joined the business. Named after his grandfather, he became sole owner in 1904. He continued to run the business until his retirement in 1924.

Right
Height: 9 inches
Marked: L. Norton/Bennington

A simple cobalt blue floral motif was brushed on this early ovoid crock with a slightly flaring collar.

The crock was made by the Bennington potteries during the years 1828 to 1833, when Luman Norton was in charge.

PHOTO 38

Height: 13¼ inches
Marked: Swan & States/Stonington

Cobalt blue highlights were brushed at the terminal points of the handles and over the maker's mark on this ovoid crock.

Joshua Swan, Jr., and Ichabod States, of the Connecticut family of potters, operated their shop c. 1823 to 1835.

PHOTO 39

Height: 10 inches
Marked: Julius Norton/Bennington, Vt.

A small cobalt blue rabbit leaps across the front of this slightly ovoid crock.

The maker's mark represents the years from 1847 through 1850 in the operation of the Bennington potteries.

PHOTO 40

Left
Height: 9 inches
Marked: Whites, Utica

An elaborate cobalt blue floral design decorates this tapered, ovoid crock.

Noah White established his pottery in Utica, New York, in 1838. Succeeding generations ran it until 1909. The maker's mark on this jug was used from 1865 to 1877.

Right
Height: 7 inches
Marked: White & Wood/Binghamton, N.Y.

The heavily brushed cobalt blue design is a simple leaf pattern.

Charles N. White, grandson of the Utica, New York, potter Noah White, and George H. Wood were the proprietors of the White & Wood pottery of Binghamton, New York, from 1882 until 1888.

These crocks appear in color on page 22.

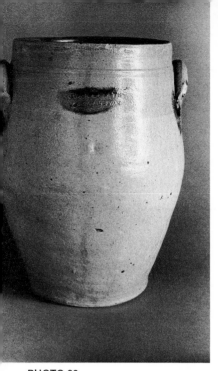

PHOTO 38

PHOTO 39

PHOTO 40

PHOTO 41

PHOTO 42

PHOTO 43

PHOTO 41
Height: 10 inches
Marked: Ottman Bros./Fort Edward, N.Y.

This crock is decorated with a chicken pecking corn, in cobalt blue.

William R. and Gilbert Ottman operated their pottery in Fort Edward, New York, from 1872 to c. 1892.

PHOTO 42
Height: 11 inches
Marked: Whites, Utica

A cobalt blue fantail bird design decorates this crock.

Noah White established his pottery in Utica, New York, in 1838. Succeeding generations ran it until 1909. The maker's mark on this jug was used from 1865 to 1877.

PHOTO 43
Left
Height: 10 inches
Marked: F. B. Norton & Co./Worcester, Mass.

A heavily brushed cobalt blue bird is perched on a leafy branch on this crock.

Franklin Blackmer Norton operated a pottery in Worcester, Massachusetts, from 1858 to 1885. This mark represents the years c. 1865 to 1885.

Right
Height: 9 inches
Marked: Lamson & Swasey/Portland, Me.

A bird perched on a branch done in cobalt blue decorates this crock.

Rufus Lamson and Eben Swasey established a pottery in Portland, Maine, in 1875. They started to produce stoneware in 1881, when the firm became known as the Portland Pottery Works. The maker's mark represents the years from 1875 to c. 1884.

PHOTO 44

Height: 12 inches
Marked: O. L. & A. K. Ballard/Burlington, Vt.

This crock is decorated with an elaborate cobalt blue fruit motif, in the form of a bunch of grapes.

O. L. and A. K. Ballard operated a pottery in Burlington, Vermont, from 1856 to 1867.

PHOTO 45

Height: 10 inches
Marked: Adam Caire/Pokeepsie, N.Y.

The elaborate cobalt blue decoration on this crock shows a bird perched on a tree stump.

Adam Caire was the youngest son of John B. Caire, who established a pottery in Poughkeepsie, New York, in 1842. The maker's mark represents the last years of the Caire pottery, 1878 to 1896.

◄ PHOTO 44

PHOTO 45

PHOTO 46
Height: 10½ inches
Marked: T. Harrington/Lyons

A script-written three-gallon capacity mark is on either side of the large cobalt blue flower design on this crock.

Thompson Harrington operated a branch of the pottery of Nathan Clark, of Athens, New York, in Lyons, New York, from 1826. He became sole owner in 1852 and continued to operate it until 1872.

PHOTO 47
Height: 11 inches
Marked: White & Wood/Binghamton, N.Y.

The decoration on this crock consists of a heavy cobalt blue leaf design combined with a Spencerian script motif.

Charles N. White, grandson of the Utica, New York, potter Noah White, and George H. Wood operated the White & Wood pottery of Binghamton, New York, from 1882 until 1888.

PHOTO 48
Left
Height: 10 inches
Marked: Riedinger & Caire/Poughkeepsie

This cobalt blue leaf design is typical of the decoration found on many New York State pieces.

Philip Riedinger and Adam Caire used this maker's mark on their pieces from 1857 to 1878. The pottery was in Poughkeepsie, New York.

Right
Height: 8 inches
Marked: Cortland

The cobalt blue nonrepresentational design on this crock is typical of those done by the Woodruff pottery decorators of Cortland, New York.

This crock is attributed to Madison Woodruff, who operated his pottery in Cortland, New York, from 1849 to c. 1885.

PHOTO 46

PHOTO 47

PHOTO 48

PHOTO 49

PHOTO 50

PHOTO 51

PHOTO 49

Height: 11 inches
Marked: E. & L. P. Norton/Bennington, Vt.

A large, heavily brushed leaf design surrounded by dots in cobalt blue decorates this crock.

The Bennington potteries used this maker's mark during the years from 1861 to 1881.

PHOTO 50

Height: 7 inches
No Maker's Mark

This crock was made for a wholesale purchaser. Written in cobalt blue script is "Tompkins & Welsh, Morristown, N.J."

PHOTO 51

Height: 7¾ inches, 8 inches
Marked: D. Weston/Ellenville, N.Y.

Both crocks are decorated with cobalt blue lilaclike flowers done in Spencerian swirls.

Horace Weston established his pottery in Ellenville, New York, in 1829. His son Daniel took over the operation of the pottery in 1849. The maker's mark shown here was used from 1849 until Daniel's retirement c. 1875.

PHOTO 52

Height: 11 inches
Marked: C. Hart/Sherburne

A leaf with two polka-dot-decorated flowers in cobalt blue forms the floral motif on this crock.

James Hart established a pottery in Sherburne, New York, in 1841 with his son Charles. James retired in 1858 and Charles operated the pottery alone until 1866 when he was joined by his son Nahum. This maker's mark represents the years from 1858 until 1866, during which Charles was sole owner.

PHOTO 52

PHOTO 53

PHOTO 54

PHOTO 53

Height: 8¾ inches
Marked: Seymour Brothers/Hartford

A cobalt blue star decorates this crock.

The Seymour family of Hartford, Connecticut, used this maker's mark from 1867 to c. 1871.

PHOTO 54

Left
Height: 9 inches
Marked: Jacob Zipf/Union Pottery/Newark, N.J.

Two large brushed flowers decorate this crock. The two-gallon capacity mark is script-written.

Conrad Haidle and John C. Sonn started the Union Pottery in 1871. Jacob Zipf joined the pottery in 1875. Pieces from this period are marked "Haidle and Zipf." Zipf became sole owner in 1877. His company operated in Newark, New Jersey, from 1877 to 1906.

Right
Height: 8 inches
Marked: Fulper Bros./Flemington, N.J.

A simple cobalt blue leaf design decorates this crock.

The Fulper Pottery Company was founded by Abraham Fulper in Flemington, New Jersey, in 1805. The majority of their stoneware was produced from 1840 to 1910. The company, now called Stangl Pottery, is still in operation.

PHOTO 55

Height: 10½ inches, 8¾ inches
Marked: Gardiner Stone Ware/Manufactory/Gardiner, Me.

The eagle that was used to decorate one of these crocks was impressed with a stamp. The design embossed in relief on the stamp was impressed into the wet clay before the crock was fired. The swan design was also stamped into the clay before firing, with a stamp that had been dipped into a cobalt blue glaze first. These pieces should not be confused with the early nineteenth-century stamp-impressed pieces.

The Gardiner Stone Ware Manufactory was in operation in Gardiner, Maine, from c. 1874 to 1887.

PHOTO 56

Left
Height: 7¼ inches
No Maker's Mark

This butter crock was made for a Chicago company. The lid sits in a recessed rim and a wire bail handle with a wooden grip is attached to pottery loops. Imprinted in cobalt blue is the inscription "5 Lbs. Net Hazel Extra Creamery Butter Is Guaranteed to Conform in All Respects With National Pure Food Laws. Hazel Pure Food Company, Chicago."

Center
Height: 7¼ inches
No Maker's Mark

Imprinted in black on this butter crock is the inscription "Net Weight 5 Pounds, Fountain Quality Special Creamery Butter. J. B. Greenhut Company, New York." The lid of the crock fits into a recessed rim. A wire bail handle with a wooden grip is attached to pottery loops.

Greenhut Department Store was located at 294-301 Sixth Avenue in the Chelsea section of New York City c. 1915.

Right
Height: 7¼ inches
No Maker's Mark

This butter crock was made for a wholesale purchaser. Its lid sits in a recessed rim. Originally, a wire bail handle was attached to the pottery loops on the sides of the crock. Imprinted in black is the inscription "5 Lbs. Net, Royal Stuart Extra Creamery Butter, Simpson Crawford Co., Sixth Avenue, 19th to 20th Sts., New York." Simpson Crawford was a department store in the Chelsea section of New York City c. 1915.

PHOTO 55

PHOTO 56

Jars

Jars were wide-mouthed containers, generally narrower than crocks. They were used for preserving and storing foods. Jars can be found with or without handles, and were made in both ovoid and cylindrical shapes; the cylindrical, straight-sided form was more common.

Early food preserving jars were sealed with lard and covered with cheesecloth, while later nineteenth-century pieces had an inset rim that was covered with a tin or wooden lid and sealed with wax. In 1892 a preserve jar with a wire lever that secured the lid was patented. A stoneware Mason jar was also made that featured a zinc screw cap with a glass liner.

Storage jars were made with stoneware lids that either fit into a recessed ridge or rested on top of the rim. Most storage and preserve jars were made in sizes from a quarter gallon to six gallons.

PHOTO 57
Height: 10¾ inches
No Maker's Mark

An incised leaf design typical of John Remmey III is repeated on both sides of this jar. The leaves were brushed with cobalt blue.

This preserve jar is attributed to John Remmey III, who operated his family's pottery c. 1791 to c. 1831. His grandfather, the first John Remmey, arrived in Manhattan from Germany about 1731 and established a pottery c. 1735. His son, John Remmey, Jr., operated the pottery until his death in 1792. *His* sons, Henry and John III, had joined the business in 1791. Henry left to found his own pottery in Pennsylvania, leaving John III to operate the Remmey pottery, which was last listed in the New York City Directories in 1831.

PHOTO 57

PHOTO 58

Height: 9¼ inches
Marked: Nichols & Boynton/Burlington, Vt.

A dark cobalt blue leaflike motif decorates this jar. There is a lid which fits into the recessed rim.

The Nichols and Alford pottery was established in 1854. From 1856 to c. 1859 the company was called Nichols and Boynton.

PHOTO 59

Height: 11 inches
Marked: Wm. A. MacQuoid & Co./New-York/Little Wst 12th St.

This jar is decorated with two flowers freely brushed on in cobalt blue. There is a lid which fits into a recessed rim and there are two handles, typical of those used on crocks.

William MacQuoid bought the pottery works of Lewis Lehman on West 12th Street, New York City, in 1863. He ran the pottery until 1879.

PHOTO 60

Height: 10¼ inches
Marked: Pottery Works/(three impressed stars)/Little Wst 12th St., N.Y.

A cobalt blue daisy decorates this two-handled jar. The lid fits into a recessed rim.

This maker's mark was used by William MacQuoid from 1863 to 1879.

PHOTO 61

Height: 11 inches
Marked: A. K. Ballard/Burlington, Vt.

A cobalt blue loop design decorates this two-handled jar. A lid fits into the recessed rim.

The firm of O. L. & A. K. Ballard took over the Nichols and Boynton pottery about 1859. By c. 1867 the initials O. L. were dropped and A. K. Ballard operated the pottery until 1872.

PHOTO 58

PHOTO 59

PHOTO 62

Left
Height: 11 inches
Marked: S. L. Pewtress & Co. /New Haven, Conn.

The cobalt blue decoration on this jar is a stylized leaf design. The handles are crock type, and a missing cover fit into the recessed rim.

S. L. Pewtress started his New Haven, Connecticut, pottery c. 1868. George Henderson, who later founded the Dorchester Pottery Works in Massachusetts, became manager in 1880. The pottery was in operation until 1887.

Right
Height: 10 inches
Marked: A. O. Whittemore/Havana, N.Y.

A cobalt blue floral motif decorates this jar, which has crock-type handles. A missing cover fit into the recessed rim.

Albert O. Whittemore operated his pottery in Havana, New York (now called Montour Falls), from 1869 to c. 1893.

PHOTO 60

PHOTO 61

PHOTO 63 ►

PHOTO 62

PHOTO 64

PHOTO 65

PHOTO 63

Height: 10½ inches
Marked: J. & E. Norton/Bennington, Vt.

A complex flower motif, a typical design of the period, decorates this two-handled jar. A lid which fit into the recessed rim is missing.

This mark represents the years between 1850 and 1859 in the production of the Bennington potteries. During this period some of the most elaborate and well-executed designs were made.

PHOTO 64

Left
Height: 9½ inches
Marked: Hamilton & Jones/Greensboro/Pa.

The name and address of the maker is stenciled in cobalt blue on this jar.

James Hamilton had a brother, Leet, who was also a potter in the Greensboro, Pennsylvania, area. Leet's son-in-law joined him to form a company called Hamilton and Jones c. 1880.

Center
Height: 12¼ inches
Marked: S. Bell & Sons/Strasburg.

A leaf motif placed just below the top rim circles this preserve jar.

The maker's mark represents the years from 1882 to 1908 during the operation of the Bell pottery of Strasburg, Virginia.

Right
Height: 9½ inches
Marked: Jas. Hamilton/& Co./Greensboro/Pa.

The name and address of the maker was stenciled in cobalt blue on this preserve jar. The inset rim had a lid of either tin or wood that was sealed on with wax.

James Hamilton operated a pottery in Greensboro, Pennsylvania, from sometime in the 1850s until 1880.

PHOTO 65

Left and Right
Height: 8 inches, 7 inches
Marked: The Weir Pat. March 1st 92 April 16th 1901

Weir preserve jars were made in sizes from one pint to ten gallons. The Weir mark was embossed around the lid, which was secured by a wire lever. An advertisement for the Weir jar in *The Ladies' Home Journal* of July 1902 stated that "Heinz, the pickle man, has just ordered 500,000 Weir Jars."

The Weir Pottery Company of Monmouth, Illinois, was incorporated in September 1899 to manufacture the jar invented by William Weir. Weir was one of several companies that merged to form the Western Stoneware Company in 1906.

Center
Height: 9 inches
Marked: Western Stoneware Company, Monmouth Illinois, #5 Weir Seal

The maker's mark was embossed around the lid of this preserve jar. A wire handle with a lever secured the lid in place. Impressed on the base of the jar are the numbers "150 52."

The Western Stoneware Company was formed in 1906 by the merger of the Monmouth Pottery Company, the Weir Pottery Company, both of Monmouth, Illinois, the Macomb Stoneware Company, the Macomb Pottery Company, both of Macomb, Illinois, the Whitehall Pottery Company of White Hall, Illinois, the Fort Dodge Pottery Company of Iowa, and the Clinton Pottery Company of Missouri. Western Stoneware is still in operation in Monmouth, Illinois.

PHOTO 66

Height: 9¾ inches
No Maker's Mark

An open loop handle typical of those found on jugs is attached to this preserve jar. The mouth has an inset rim. Stenciled in cobalt blue are the words "W. L. Walpole, Roseville, O."

PHOTO 66

◄ PHOTO 67

PHOTO 68

PHOTO 69

PHOTO 67
Height: 6¾ inches
Marked: Peoria

Cast in a mold, the lower portion of this preserve jar has twelve vertical panels. The mouth has an inset rim which had either a wooden or metal lid. Both the interior and the exterior are coated with a dark brown slip.

This jar was made in Illinois by the Peoria Pottery Company, which operated from 1873 to 1902.

PHOTO 68
Left
Height: 8¾ inches
No Maker's Mark

The wholesale purchaser Demuth had this snuff jar made for his product. Imprinted in black is "Demuth's Celebrated Snuff, Established 1770, Lancaster, Pa." The cover fits into a recessed rim.

Right
Height: 5½ inches
No Maker's Mark

Imprinted in blue is "Standard Ink Co., Buffalo, N.Y.," the wholesale purchaser of this ink jar. The cover fits into a recessed rim.

PHOTO 69
Height: 7¼ inches, 7¼ inches
Marked: The Weir Pat'd Mar. 1st 1892

The dome-shaped lid and the shoulder of each of these Weir preserve jars are coated with brown slip. The Weir mark is embossed on the lid, which was secured with a wire lever.

The Weir Pottery Company of Monmouth, Illinois, was incorporated September 28, 1899, to manufacture the stone fruit jar invented by William S. Weir.

PHOTO 70

PHOTO 70

Height: 7 inches
Marked: Union/Stoneware Co./Red Wing, Minn.

The zinc screw cap on this preserve jar, invented by John L. Mason and widely used by the glass industry, was adapted by the Union Stoneware Company for their Stone Mason Fruit Jar. This name and the name and location of the pottery are imprinted in black on the jar. Impressed on the base of the jar is "Pat. Jan. 24, 1899."

PHOTO 71

Height: 9½ inches
No Maker's Mark

This jar was made for the Sanford Ink Company. Imprinted in blue is "Sanford's Inks—The Dependable Line—Pastes—Illegal to Refill This Jar for Resale." The lid is secured with a wire lever handle and a second wire bail handle with a wooden grip was attached to make it easier to carry. Impressed on the base are the numbers "150 52," which can be found on similar pieces made by the Western Stoneware Company of Monmouth, Illinois.

PHOTO 71

Bottles

Bottles were cylindrical containers with small mouths that could be sealed with cork. They kept liquids cold and insulated. Stoneware bottles were used most often in taverns and stores before refrigeration was common.

A variety of cylindrical bottle shapes were made until the mid-1850s. After this, bottles were pressed or molded, and they were made with straight or slightly tapering sides, a cone-shaped neck, and a heavy lip.

Stoneware bottles were made in quantity for brewers, taverns, and merchants, rather than for individuals. They held alcoholic beverages, soda, beer, ink, medicine, acid, and vulcanizing fluid.

Very few pieces were decorated or had maker's marks. Occasionally, they had a wash of blue or brown slip around the top or shoulder. Many bottles had names or initials impressed on them. Most often this represented the name of the merchant who purchased the bottle rather than the name of the potter. Late nineteenth-century examples have imprinted names and symbols on them.

Most stoneware bottles were made in a one-quart size, with pint and two-quart containers uncommon. Late nineteenth-century bottles are more readily found in pint sizes.

PHOTO 72
Height: 10½ inches
No Maker's Mark

The name "Post" in cobalt blue is on the shoulder of this bottle. Post's root beer was made in Poughkeepsie during the late nineteenth century.

It is believed that these pieces were made at the Caire Pottery in Poughkeepsie, New York, c. 1878 until 1896.

PHOTO 72

PHOTO 73

Left
Height: 9¾ inches
No Maker's Mark

The name of the wholesale purchaser, "D. L. Ormsby," and the date "1847" have been impressed on this bottle. Ormsby brewed beer and root beer and manufactured soda water. In 1847 he was located in New York City, at 255 West 16th Street.

Center
Height: 10 inches
No Maker's Mark

Impressed on this bottle is the message "J. M. & G. I. Hager, Dealers in Hardware & Paint, Burlington, Vt." The bottle may have been used for turpentine, varnish, or linseed oil.

Right
Height: 10 inches
Marked: W. Smith

This twelve-sided bottle is impressed "Patent, Pressed, W. Smith." Also impressed are the wholesale purchaser's name, "D. L. Ormsby," and the date "1849."

Washington Smith established his pottery in 1833 at 32-34 Eighteenth Street, Manhattan. His son Washington I. Smith joined the business in 1861. They operated the business together until 1863 when Washington Smith retired, leaving his son to operate the pottery until it was sold in 1870.

Pieces with the maker's marks of Goodwin and Webster, of Connecticut, and Cowden and Wilcox, of Pennsylvania, have been found on the Smith patent bottle.

PHOTO 74

Left
Height: 10 inches
No Maker's Mark

A dark brown glaze has been brushed from the top of the lip to the shoulder line of this bottle. It was made for the whole-

PHOTO 73

PHOTO 74

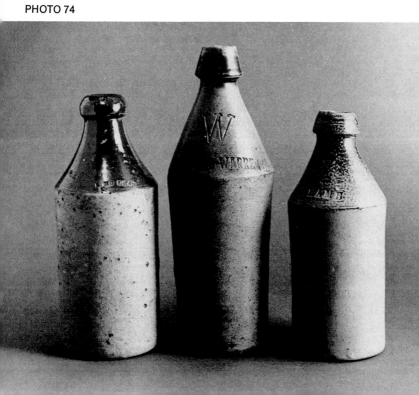

PHOTO 75

PHOTO 76

sale purchaser "S. McLean," whose name was impressed on the shoulder.

Center
Height: 11½ inches
No Maker's Mark

The lip and shoulder of this bottle have been brushed with a dark brown glaze. A large "W" was impressed on the shoulder, above the name of the wholesale purchaser: "Richard Warren Co." Richard Warren was a manufacturer of mineral water and a bottler of lager, porter, ale, and cider. His company was located in Paterson, New Jersey, c. 1884 to c. 1899.

Right
Height: 9¼ inches
No Maker's Mark

A brown glaze was brushed on the lip and shoulder of this bottle. The wholesale purchaser's name, "J. Lamb," was impressed on one side and on the reverse, "Root Beer."

PHOTO 75

Left
Height: 10¾ inches
No Maker's Mark

A cobalt blue script-written "B" is on either side of the impressed wholesale purchaser's name: "P. Pfannbecker." Pfannbecker was a bottler and manufacturer of birch, spruce, and ginger beer in Paterson, New Jersey, c. 1870 to c. 1918.

Center
Height: 9¾ inches
No Maker's Mark

A large cobalt blue "A" was brushed on this bottle. No other marks have been impressed.

Right
Height: 11 inches
No Maker's Mark

The letter "W" is script-written twice in cobalt blue on this otherwise unmarked bottle. Brown slip highlights the lip.

PHOTO 76

Left
Height: 11 inches
No Maker's Mark

The names "Tiffany & Allen" have been impressed on the shoulder of this bottle. The lip has been highlighted with cobalt blue.

Charles Tiffany and William T. Allen were manufacturers of mineral waters. They were located in the Washington Market, Paterson, New Jersey, from c. 1877 to c. 1890.

Center
Height: 10½ inches
No Maker's Mark

A band of cobalt blue was brushed around the shoulder of this bottle, which has been impressed with the wholesale purchaser's name: "Sal Josephs P.N.J."

Right
Height: 10 inches
No Maker's Mark

The wholesale purchaser's name, "S. Sickerts," has been impressed on this bottle. Cobalt blue was brushed from the top of the lip to the shoulder.

PHOTO 77

Height: 6 inches
No Maker's Mark

The only marks on this flattened flask are the rings incised in the clay at the neck of the bottle.

Although stoneware flasks were usually ovoid-shaped bottles with a flattened front and back, some were made in rounded and rectangular shapes. Other unusual flasks had handles. However, flasks in any shape are rare.

PHOTO 77

PHOTO 78

PHOTO 79

PHOTO 78

Left
Height: 8 inches
No Maker's Mark

A horse and the brewer's name and city have been impressed on this beer bottle made for I. S. Meister, Milwaukee.

This bottle is attributed to the Hermann Pottery of Milwaukee, Wisconsin, which operated from 1856 to 1902.

Center
Height: 8¾ inches
No Maker's Mark

This bottle is covered with a dark brown glaze. Impressed is the name and address of the wholesale purchaser: "Lyons Delany Co., Pawtucket, R.I."

Right
Height: 7½ inches
No Maker's Mark

Impressed on this bottle is "Adrian Feyh, 266 William Street, New York, 1873." Feyh, a brewer, was located at the William Street address from 1856 to c. 1893.

PHOTO 79

Left
Height: 7½ inches
No Maker's Mark

This bottle was made for a wholesale purchaser. Imprinted is "F. Sandkuhler's Trade Mark Registered Superior Weiss Beer Brewery, 109 N. Collington Ave., Baltimore." Frank Sandkuhler opened a brewery in 1879. He was at the above address from 1898 until 1919 when the brewery closed.

Center
Height: 10¾ inches
No Maker's Mark

This bottle was made for Grumman's Bottling Works. Imprinted in the center of two circles on the bottle is a large "G

Estb 1844." Imprinted around the second circle is "Grumman's Bottling Works, So. Norwalk, Conn." Pieces with "H.J. & G.S. Grumman" impressed on the shoulder can also be found.

Right
Height: 7¼ inches
No Maker's Mark

Imprinted in black on this ginger beer bottle is "The Original Brew 'With a Pedigree' Diamond A English Brewed Ginger Beer, Salt City Bottling Co., Syracuse, N.Y." To the left of the lettering is a black diamond shape with an "A" in the center.

PHOTO 80

Height: 8½ inches, 10¼ inches
Marked: Glasgow Pottery Co.

Imprinted in a circle on each of these beer bottles is "The Christian Moerlein Brewing Co., Cincinnati." The words "Exhilerating, Wholesome, Delicious, and Pure" are on either side of a second circle, with "Moerlein's Old Jug-Lager Krug-Bier" in the center. Below this circle are two cherubs, to the right a grape vine, and to the left a sheaf of wheat. The upper portion of each bottle is coated with an ochre glaze.

Christian Moerlein's brewery opened in 1853 and remained in business until 1919.

The impressed oval mark at the base of the bottle represents the Glasgow Pottery Company, Trenton, New Jersey, which operated from 1860 until 1890.

PHOTO 81

Left
Height: 5 inches
No Maker's Mark

The wholesale purchaser's product and name are imprinted

PHOTO 80

PHOTO 81

PHOTO 82

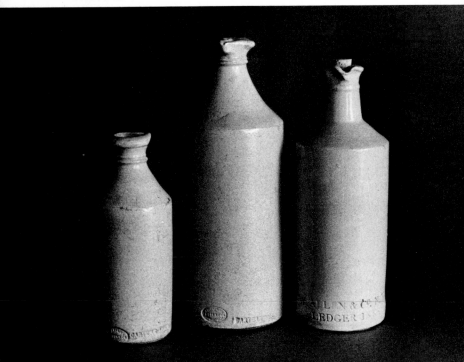

in black on this vulcanizing fluid bottle. The message reads "Vulcanizing Fluid C. O. T. Co., Tingley, Rahway, N.J."

Center
Height: 8 inches
No Maker's Mark

Imprinted in black are the words "Vulcanizing Solution. Mfd. by the M. & M. Mfg. Co., Akron, Ohio." This bottle, which contained a vulcanizing solution, was made for a wholesale purchaser.

Right
Height: 5 inches
No Maker's Mark

The wholesale purchaser's name and product are imprinted in black on this bottle. The message reads "Acid for Half and Half Cement, The Manhattan Rubber Mfg. Co., Passaic, N.J." The Manhattan Rubber Manufacturing Company first appeared in 1901 in the Passaic City Directories.

PHOTO 82

Left and Center
Height: 6¼ inches, 9½ inches
Marked: Enterprise Pottery Co., New Brighton, Pa.

These large ink bottles with pouring spouts are called master inks and were used for the bulk storage of ink. Impressed on these bottles is the name of the wholesale purchaser, "Carter's Ink," as well as the potter's name and address, the "Enterprise Pottery Co., New Brighton, Pa."

The Enterprise Pottery Company was in operation from c. 1880 until 1900.

Right
Height: 8 inches
No Maker's Mark

"W. Allen & Co., N.Y., Ledger Inks" is impressed on this master ink bottle, made for a wholesale purchaser.

Batter Jugs

Batter jugs or pails were slightly ovoid, wide-mouthed jugs with a tubular pouring spout, used to mix and pour pancake batter. Tin covers or lids were made to fit the mouth and spout.

Early batter jugs had two rounded stand-up handles at the sides. Most of the pieces available today have a wire bail handle with a wooden grip, which is attached at either side of the mouth through pottery loops. These later examples also have a crock handle added to the lower part of the back to make pouring easier.

Although decorated pieces were made, most batter jugs were plain and unmarked. They are most frequently found in three-quarter-gallon, one-gallon, and one-and-a-half-gallon sizes.

PHOTO 83
Height: 8 inches
No Maker's Mark

Wide bands of cobalt blue are brushed around the spout and the handle on the back of this slightly ovoid batter jug. The tin lids for the spout and the mouth are missing.

PHOTO 84
Left
Height: 8 inches
Marked: N. White & Co., Binghamton

Cobalt blue has been brushed around the spout and handles of this batter jug. The maker's mark is impressed on the back of the neck. Originally, there were tin lids on the mouth and spout of the jug, and there was also a wire bail handle, all of which are now missing.

William Roberts operated a pottery in Binghamton, New

PHOTO 83

York, in association with his father-in-law Noah White, the Utica, New York, potter. Maker's marks with either White's or Roberts's name can be found. This mark was used by them during the years 1865 to 1868.

Center
Height: 8¾ inches
No Maker's Mark

This unmarked batter jug is decorated with a simple cobalt blue leaf design. The original wire bail handle is attached and there is a tin lid covering the spout. However, the lid for the mouth is missing.

Right
Height: 8¾ inches
Marked: W. Roberts, Binghamton, N.Y.

The spout and handles of this batter jug are highlighted with cobalt blue. The maker's mark is impressed on the back of the neck. The original wire bail handle is attached, but the tin lids for the mouth and the spout are missing.

William Roberts operated a pottery in Binghamton, New York, with various members of the White family, potters from Utica, New York. This maker's mark was used during the years 1848 to 1888.

PHOTO 84

PHOTO 85

PHOTO 85
Height: 11½ inches, 8½ inches
No Maker's Mark

These slightly ovoid batter jugs have a molded three-leaf design forming the pottery loops by which the wire bail handle was attached.

An illustration of this style appears on the 1903 price list published by the Robinson Clay Product Company of Ohio, and on a list published in 1899 by the Syracuse Stoneware Company of Syracuse, New York. This price list included the addresses of their office and warehouses, 401 to 417 Fulton Street, Syracuse, and their factories in Akron, Ohio. This company was in operation from 1891 to c. 1915 and may have been a wholesaler for an Ohio pottery manufacturer rather than a producer of its own wares.

Churns

Churns were tall, either slightly tapered or straight-sided containers that were used for making butter. Many were made with typical crock handles. They came with stoneware or wooden lids that had an opening for the dasher in the center. These lids were used to keep the cream from splashing out and to hold the dasher in place. The dasher was a wooden pole the size of a broomstick that extended several feet above the rim of the churn and had a disk at its base. It was steadily pushed up and down in a partially cream-filled churn to make the butter.

Generally, churns are hard to find, especially decorated and marked examples. They were made in two-gallon, three-gallon, four-gallon, five-gallon, six-gallon, eight-gallon, ten-gallon, and twelve-gallon sizes.

PHOTO 86

Left
Height: 18½ inches
Marked: W. Roberts, Binghamton, N.Y.

This slightly tapered butter churn was decorated with a cobalt blue floral design. The stoneware lid has an opening in the center for the wooden dasher.

William Roberts operated a pottery in Binghamton, New York, from 1848 until his death in 1888.

Right
Height: 15 inches
No Maker's Mark

A cobalt blue flower and leaf design decorates this slightly tapered churn. It has crock-type handles, for lifting, and a stoneware lid.

PHOTO 86

PHOTO 87

Height: 15 inches
Marked: Red Wing/Union Stoneware Co./Red Wing, Minn.

Imprinted on this churn in cobalt blue is the six-gallon capacity mark and "Red Wing, Union Stoneware Co., Red Wing, Minnesota." The Red Wing trademark (a wing) is imprinted in red. The churn has a wooden lid and dasher.

The Red Wing Stoneware Company was formed in 1877. Although it stopped making stoneware c. 1949, the company continued to make tableware and other pottery until it closed in 1967.

PHOTO 87

Pitchers

Pitchers were cylindrical containers with pouring spouts and handles used for keeping and serving liquids such as water, milk, cream, and stews. Most early pitchers had a bulbous body that tapered into the neck. The spout was formed by being pulled out from the neck. The handle was applied after the body was shaped. Later pitchers were made in straight-sided cylindrical forms. Many were glazed all over with Albany slip, which was a brown coating.

Decorated, marked stoneware pitchers are hard to find. Most pitchers were made in quarter-gallon, half-gallon, one-and-a-half-gallon, and two-gallon sizes.

PHOTO 88
Height: 9¾ inches
Marked: F. T. Wright & Son/Taunton, Mass

The only decorations on this attractively shaped pitcher are the impressed lines that run around the collar and shoulder.

Franklin T. Wright operated his pottery in Taunton, Massachusetts, from 1855 to 1868. This mark first appeared in the 1860s, when Wright's son joined the company.

PHOTO 89 (see page 15)
Height: 12½ inches
No Maker's Mark

This unmarked pitcher is decorated with the bird-on-the-branch motif. Its bulbous shape curves into a straight neck with a pulled-out spout. The rim has a one-inch collar.

PHOTO 88

Collecting, Purchasing, Care, and Display

COLLECTING

The earliest stoneware appeals to collectors of early Americana. The late nineteenth-century and early twentieth-century pieces, which were mass-produced, appeal to collectors of nostalgia who wish to preserve items from the more recent past. Since crocks, jugs, jars, and bottles were produced in the greatest quantity, they are the most available. Pieces with maker's marks are more sought after than those that are unmarked. Remember that the names found on the pieces are not necessarily those of the maker; they may represent the merchant for whom the piece was made. Any design of a historical character or any reference to a local or national event gives a piece special value. The rarest pieces are those that show the most original or unusual designs.

Small stoneware utensils such as inkwells, porringers, and mugs have become appealing collector's items, although most of these pieces are not heavily decorated or marked. True miniatures in stoneware are very unusual. They may have been made as toys, samples, or souvenirs. Small banks and whistles were made for children.

RESEARCH

Owners of American stoneware often do research about the period to which their pieces belong. This research and documentation frequently involves finding and examining price lists, advertising, and order forms of the original stoneware

Facing page: Stoneware pieces make attractive containers for dried floral arrangements. The crock in the center was made by Hamilton & Jones, of Greensboro, Pennsylvania. Quarter-gallon jugs, like the smaller pieces here, are hard to find.

manufacturers. Most stoneware potteries distributed price lists and order forms which gave the full line of pottery being made. Some lists featured pictures of the items that were being sold. These documents are interesting not only because of the historical information they contain but also as rarities themselves.

PURCHASING

Before purchasing stoneware it is useful to visit local museums, historical societies, and dealers in Americana where marked and documented pieces from the earliest times can be seen and studied. They will help acquaint you with fine examples of stoneware that are not readily available. Attending antique shows and visiting antique shops will show you what is available and give you some idea of the prices these pieces command.

When you are ready to buy, visit local dealers, flea markets, small thrift shops, and shows in your area; these are good sources for locally made stoneware. Ads in newspapers and

---

Facing page: An illustrated stoneware price list dated 1866

An advertisement from *The Ladies' Home Journal* of July 1902 featuring the Weir Jar, a stoneware canning jar made for preserving fruits and vegetables

The Weir Jar

makes the putting up of fruit and vegetables **a pleasure.** So easy when all is ready, to fill the jar and simply press a lever to seal it airtight. When cool, you make our **air-tight test** (booklet tells about it) and you **know** the contents will keep indefinitely. No light gets in and this guarantees the flavor and color. Beautiful results with strawberries and the like.

WEIR JARS of earthenware enameled inside and out, are made in pint to ten gallon sizes; **they never break;** are cheapest in the end; and the **best dealers sell them.**

Every housekeeper should have our free booklet containing recipes, the air-tight test, and complete description of the Weir Jars and their use. Sent for your grocer's name.

WEIR POTTERY COMPANY, 200 Main St., Monmouth, Ill.

Heinz, the pickle man, has just ordered 500,000 Weir Jars.

WHOLESALE PRICES OF STONE-WARE.

TERMS NETT CASH FROM THIS LIST.

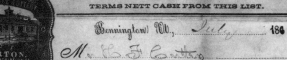

E. & L. P. NORTON,
MANUFACTURERS OF EVERY DESCRIPTION OF
STONE WARE
BENNINGTON VT.

Bennington, Vt., _July_ 186 6

M. H. F. Cutting

Bo't of **E. & L. P. NORTON,**

ORDERS BY MAIL PROMPTLY ATTENDED TO.

EDWARD NORTON,   LUMAN P. NORTON.

JUGS.

	Per Dozen.
Doz. 4 Gallon,	$10,00
" 3 "	8,00
" 2 "	6,00
" 1 1-2 "	4,50
" 1 "	3,50
" 1-2 "	2,50
" 1-4 "	1,50
" 1-8 "	1,00

MOLASSES JUGS.

Doz. 2 Gallon,	6,50
" 1 "	4,00
" 1-2 "	2,75

OPEN POTS, Cream or Butter.

Doz. 6 Gallon,	14,00
" 5 "	12,00
" 4 "	10,00
" 3 "	8,00
" 2 "	6,00
" 1 1-2 "	4,50
" 1 "	3,50

COVERED CREAM POTS

Doz. 4 Gallon,	12,00
" 3 "	9,50
" 2 "	7,00
" 1 1-2 "	5,50
" 1 "	4,50

CHURNS.

Doz. 6 Gallon,	15,00
" 5 "	13,00
" 4 "	11,00
" 3 "	9,00
" 2 "	7,00

COVERED PRESERVE JARS.

Doz. 4 Gallon,	10,00
" 3 "	8,00
" 2 "	6,00
" 1 1-2 "	5,25
" 1 "	4,00
" 1-2 "	2,75
" 1-4 "	1,75

FRUIT OR TOMATO JARS.

Doz. 1-2 Gallon, with corks,	3,00
" 1-4 "	2,00
Bean Pots, Doz. 1 Gallon,	3,50
" 1-2 "	2,50
Pudding Pots, Doz. 1 Gallon,	3,50
" 1-2 "	2,50
Chambers, Doz. 1st size,	3,50
" 2d "	2,50
Beer Bottles, per doz.,	1,25
Quart Mugs, " "	1,50
Pint " "	1,00
Water Kegs, per gallon,	0,40

BUTTER POTS, COVERED.

	Per Dozen.	
Doz. 6 Gallons,	$16,00	4 00
" 5 "	14,00	3 50
" 4 "	12,00	3 00
" 3 "	9,50	2 37
" 2 "	7,00	3 50
" 1 1-2 "	5,50	
" 1 "	4,50	2 25
" 1-2 "	3,50	1 75

COVERED CAKE POTS.

Doz. 4 Gallon,	12,00
" 3 "	9,50
" 2 "	7,00
" 1 "	4,50

PITCHERS.

Covered Batter Pitchers, Doz. 2 Gal.	7,00
Doz. 1 1-2 gallon,	5,50
" 1 "	4,50
" 1-2 "	2,75
Common Pitchers, Doz. 2 gallon,	6,00
" 1 2 "	4,50
" 1 "	3,50
" 1-2 "	2,50
" 1-4 "	1,50

FLOWER POTS.

Doz. 4 Gallon,	10,00	
" 3 "	8,00	
" 2 "	6,00	
" 1 "	3,50	3 50
" 1-2 "	2,50	2 50
" 1-4 "	1,75	1 75
" 1-8 "	1,25	1 25

STOVE TUBES.

Doz. 1st size,	6,50
" 2d "	5,00
" 3d "	3,50

ROCKINGHAM WARE.

Large Bar Room Spittoons,	13,00	
Spittoons, No. 1 per doz.	9,00	
" 2 " "	7,50	
" 3 " "	5,00	1 50
" 4 " "	4,00	1 00
Shell Pattern, " "	5,00	

DOG HANDLED PITCHERS.

6 qt per doz.	10,00
4 " "	7,00
3 " "	5,00
2 " "	4,00

TEA POTS.

1st size, per doz.	6,00
2d " "	4,50
Chambers, per doz.	6,00
French Bed Pans, per doz.	10,00
Soap Dishes, " "	2,00

Rec'd Pay E & L P Norton
E Greenslit

31,88
3,00
$34,88

magazines devoted to antiques and collectibles are also good sources for stoneware.

CARE

Stoneware requires a minimum of care. Clean pieces with a solution of mild detergent and water. Remember that almost all stoneware shows marks of the kiln, slight imperfections, burns, and irregular areas. To repair these is an unnecessary and time-consuming task. Various resins can be used to build up missing parts, but trying to match the color of the ware is a job for a professional. It is better to leave these signs of wear and age than attempt to repair a crack, chip, or missing part yourself.

DISPLAY

Most stoneware pieces are sizable and can present storage and display problems. Specially-built shelving that can sustain their weight is one solution. Placing stoneware on the floor in attractive groupings is another. Pieces can be used as containers for dried flower arrangements. Crocks and jars with lids can be used in your kitchen as storage containers for flour, rice, tea, coffee, cereal, and other products. The charm and attractiveness of each piece will often suggest new and pleasing ways of displaying your collection, large or small.

Facing page: A toy teapot and toy bean pot are shown in this advertising poster. Toy samples could be obtained by redeeming coupons, for which Swasey charged six cents in stamps.

Potters and Potteries

This list of potters and potteries and their known operating dates was compiled from business directories, museum and historical society publications, and other recent books.

Its purpose is to help you to approximate the age of a marked piece of stoneware. This is not a complete list, since not all potters or potteries marked their ware and not all the American potteries have been researched and recorded.

If a particular entry has two non-consecutive dates, it means the pottery temporarily was not in business or used another name; if there is only one date, all that is known is that the pottery was in business at approximately that time; if there is only one date followed by a dash, the company is still in operation today.

For further references, consult the bibliography.

Adams, Allison & Co., Middlebury, OH, c. 1860

Addington, S., Utica, NY, c. 1830–38

Apley & Co., Ithaca, NY, c. 1860–c. 64

Armstrong & Wentworth, Norwich, CT, 1814–34

Atcheson, H. S., Annapolis, IN, 1841–1906

Athens Pottery, Athens, NY, 1893–1900

Atwater, Caleb & Joshua, Atwater, OH, c. 1830–40

Baird, R. S., Mogadore, OH, c. 1850

Bakewell, H. N., Wellsburg, WV, c. 1831–41

Ball & Co., J. G., Poughkeepsie, NY, c. 1820

Ballard, A. K., Burlington, VT, c. 1867–72

Ballard, O. L. & A. K., Burlington, VT, 1856–67

Bangor Stoneware Works, Bangor, ME, 1890–1916

Bauer & Co., J. A., Los Angeles, CA, c. 1890–1958

Bell, J., Waynesboro, PA, 1833–80

Bell, J. W., Waynesboro, PA, 1880–95

Bell, M.C., Cornwall, NY, c. 1830–c. 50

Bell, N. C., Cornwall, NY, c. 1834–c. 40

Bell, S., Strasburg, VA, 1833–53

Bell, S. & S., Strasburg, VA, 1853–82

Bell, Upton, Waynesboro, PA, 1895–99

Bell & Sons, S., Strasburg, VA, 1882–1908

Benjamin, Jas., Cincinnati, OH, c. 1868–c. 95

Bennett, W. H., Benton, AR, 1890–1900

Bennett & Chollar, Homer, NY, 1837–39

Bethune Pottery, Bethune, SC, c. 1870–

Bissett Pottery, Old Bridge, NJ, 1800–1850

Blair, S., Cortland, NY, 1829–35

Boone & Co., T. G., Poughkeepsie, NY, c. 1836–c. 39

Boone & Sons, T. G., Brooklyn, NY, 1842–46

Booth Bros., East Liverpool, OH, 1858–65

Boss Bros., Middlebury, OH, c. 1860

Boston Pottery Co., Boston, MA, 1878–c. 1900

Boynton, C., Albany, NY, 1818–24

Boynton, C., Troy, NY, 1829–36

Boynton, J., Albany, NY, 1816–18

Boynton & Co., C., Troy, NY, 1826–29

Brady & Craft, Ellenville, NY, c. 1881

Brady & Ryan, Ellenville, NY, c. 1887–c. 1902

Brandamore & Co., W., Ellenville, NY, c. 1850

Braun, C. W., Buffalo, NY, 1856–96

Brayton, J. F., Utica, NY, c. 1830–33

Brayton & Co., J. F., Utica, NY, 1833–c. 37

Brayton & Kellogg, Utica, NY, 1827–c. 32

Brewer, S. T., Havana, NY, 1854–60

Brewer & Halm, Havana, NY, c. 1853–54

Brown, S. C., Huntington, NY, c. 1880–c. 82

Brown & McKenzie, East River, WV, c. 1870–1900

Brown Brothers, Huntington, NY, 1863–80

Bullard, J. O., & Scott, A. F., Allston, MA, c. 1870–1909

Bundock, Henry, East Oakland, CA, 1872–c. 84

Burchfield, Adam, Pittsburgh, PA, c. 1860–65

Burger, J., Jr., Rochester, NY, 1878–90

Burger, John, Rochester, NY, 1854–67

Burger & Lang, Rochester, NY, 1871–78

Burger Bros. & Co., Rochester, NY, 1867–71

Butler & Co., A. J., New Brunswick, NJ, c. 1850–67

Caire, Adam, Poughkeepsie, NY, 1878–96

Caire, F. J., Huntington, NY, 1854–63

Caire, Jacob, Poughkeepsie, NY, 1845–48

Caire & Co., J. B., Poughkeepsie, NY, 1842–43

Caire & Co., Jacob, Poughkeepsie, NY, 1843–45

Caire & Co., John B., Poughkeepsie, NY, 1845–52

Caire Pottery, Jacob, Poughkeepsie, NY, 1852–54

Campbell, J., Utica, NY, 1825–29

Carpenter, F. (Edmands Pottery), Charlestown, MA, 1812–97

Central New York Pottery, Utica, NY, 1877–82

Chapman, J., Troy, NY, c. 1815–c. 19

Chollar, T. D., Cortland, NY, c. 1844–49

Chollar, T. D., Homer, NY, 1832–37

Chollar & Darby, Cortland, NY, 1839–c. 44

Chollar & Darby, Homer, NY, 1839–44

Clark, N., Athens, NY, 1813–29

Clark, N., Rochester, NY, c. 1841–52

Clark, N., Jr., Athens, NY, 1843–91

Clark & Co., Lyons, NY, 1822–52

Clark & Co., J., Troy, NY, c. 1826–27

Clark & Co., N., Lyons, NY, 1822–52

Clark & Co., N., Mount Morris, NY, 1835–46

Clark & Fox, Athens, NY, 1829–38

Cole Pottery, Seagrove, NC, 1891–1900

Commereau, Thomas H., Manhattan, NY, 1797–c. 1819

Co-operative Pottery Co., Lyons, NY, 1902–c. 4

Cowden, F. H., Harrisburg, PA, 1881–88

Cowden, J. W., Harrisburg, PA, c. 1861–70

Cowden & Son, F. H., Harrisburg, PA, 1888–1904

Cowden & Wilcox, Harrisburg, PA, 1870–81

Crafts, Martin, Nashua. NH, 1838–52

Crafts, Martin, Whately, MA, c. 1857–61

Crafts & Co., C., Whately, MA, 1845–54

Crafts & Co., Caleb, Portland, ME, c. 1835–41

Crafts Family, Whately, MA, c. 1806–61

Craven & Family, Peter, Steeds, NC, 1750–1917

Cribbs & Son, Daniel, Tuscaloosa, AL, c. 1829–90

Cribbs & Wife, Peter, Bedford, AL, c. 1865–90

Crolius, Clarkson, Manhattan, NY, c. 1794–1838

Crolius, Clarkson, Jr., Manhattan, NY, c. 1835–49

Crolius, John, Manhattan, NY, c. 1785–1808

Crolius, John, Jr., Manhattan, NY, c. 1779–1812

Crolius, John William, Manhattan, NY, c. 1728–c. 75

Crolius, William, Manhattan, NY, c. 1770–c. 79

Cushman, Paul, Albany, NY, c. 1807–33

Darrow, L. S., Baldwinsville, NY, c. 1876

Darrow & Sons, Baldwinsville, NY, c. 1855–c. 72

Davies, T. J., Bath, SC, c. 1861–65

Diedrich & Co., M., Sheboygan, WI, c. 1887–90

Dillon, Henry & Porter, Albany, NY, 1835–39

Dillon & Co., C., Albany, NY, 1834–35

Donahue Pottery, Parkersburg, WV, 1866–1908

Dorchester Pottery Works, Dorchester, MA, c. 1880–

Eagle Pottery Co., Macomb, IL, c. 1883–1900

Eastern Stoneware Factory, Sheboygan, WI, c. 1862–87

Eaton, J., & Stout, S., Washington, NJ, 1818–45

Edmands & Co., Boston, MA, c. 1812–1905

Edmands Pottery, Charlestown, MA, 1812–1905

Elverson & Sherwood, New Brighton, PA, c. 1870

Enterprise Pottery Co., New Brighton, PA, c. 1880–1900

Farrar, G. W. & J. H., Fairfax, VT, c. 1840–59

Farrar, W. H., Syracuse, NY, 1841–57

Farrington, E. W., Elmira, NY, 1887–c. 95

Farrington & Co., J., Elmira, NY, 1886–87

Fayette & Co., Utica, NY, 1833–c. 37

Fenton, J. H., Mogadore, OH, c. 1854–75

Fenton, Jonathan, Boston, MA, 1794–96

Fenton & Co., R. (L. W. Fenton), St. Johnsbury, VT, 1808–59

Fenton & Sons, Jonathan, East Dorset, VT, 1810–c. 35

Field, T. F., Utica, NY, 1828–30

Fisher, J. (Lyons Stoneware Works), Lyons, NY. c. 1882–1902

Fisher & Co., J., Lyons, NY, 1872–c. 82

Fisk & Co., D., Cleveland, OH, c. 1835–37

Fort Dodge Pottery Co., Fort Dodge, IA, c. 1885–1906

Fort Edward Pottery Co., Fort Edward, NY, 1859–61

Fort Edward Stoneware Co. (Haxstun & Co.), Fort Edward, NY, 1875–c. 82

Fox, E. S., Athens, NY, 1838–43

Fulper Bros. Pottery (Stangl Pottery), Flemington, NJ, 1805–

Furman, N., Cheesequake Creek, NJ, 1846–56

Gardiner Stone Ware Co., Gardiner, ME, c. 1874–87

Glasgow Pottery Co., Trenton, NJ, 1860–90

Goodale & Co., Daniel, Jr., Hartford, CT, 1818–30

Goodwin, Horace, & Webster, Mack, Hartford, CT, c. 1810–40

Goodwin & Sons, Seth, Hartford, CT, c. 1795–1832

Graves, D. W., Westmoreland, NY, c. 1855–c. 75

Grimstead & Stone, Waco, KY, c. 1919–22

Guy & Co., G. S., Fort Edward, NY, c. 1882–c. 85

Haidle & Co. (Union Pottery), Newark, NJ, 1871–75

Haidle & Zipf (Union Pottery), Newark, NJ, 1875–77

Hamilton & Co., Jas., Greensboro, PA, c. 1850–80

Hamilton & Jones, Greensboro, PA, c. 1880–c. 1915

Hancock, W. H. (Congress Pottery), S. Amboy, NJ, 1828–c. 40

Harrington, T., Hartford, CT, c. 1840–52

Harrington, T., Lyons, NY, 1852–72

Harrington & Burger, Rochester, NY, 1852–54

Harris, Thomas, Cuyahoga Falls, OH, 1863–c. 80

Hart, C., Sherburne, NY, 1858–66

Hart, Delos, Akron, OH, c. 1880

Hart, J., Sherburne, NY, 1850–58

Hart, J. & S., Oswego Falls, NY, 1832–40

Hart, J. J., Ogdensburgh, NY, 1869–71

Hart, S., Fulton, NY, 1840–76

Hart, W., Ogdensburgh, NY, 1858–69

Hart & Co., C., Ogdensburgh, NY, 1850–58

Hart & Son, C., Sherburne, NY, 1866–c. 85

Hart & Son, J., Sherburne, NY, 1841–50

Hart Bros., Fulton, NY, 1878–c. 95

Hastings & Belding, S. Ashfield, MA, 1850–56

Hawthorn Pottery Co., Hawthorn, PA, 1894–c. 1928

Haxstun, Ottman & Co., Fort Edward, NY, 1867–72

Haxstun & Co., Fort Edward, NY, 1857–c. 82

Heiser, J., Buffalo, NY, 1852–56

Henderson, D. & J., Jersey City, NJ, 1828–45

Hennecke & Co., C., Milwaukee, WI, 1868–95

Henry & Van Allen, Albany, NY, 1845–48

Hermann & Co., C., Milwaukee, WI, 1856–1902

Hewell Pottery, Gillsville, GA, c. 1830–1900

Higgins, A. D., Cleveland, OH, c. 1837–50

Hilton Pottery, Hickory, NC, c. 1890–1900

Hirn & Co., Joseph, St. Louis, MO, c. 1860–69

Holmes & Purdee, Dundee, NY, c. 1845–52

Holmes & Savage, Dundee, NY, 1852–c. 60

Howard & Son, W. B., Bell City, KY, c. 1870–90

Howe & Clark, Athens, NY, 1805–13

Hubbell & Chesebro, Geddes, NY, c. 1867–84

Hudson, Nathenial, Galway, NY, c. 1850–c. 66

Hudson & French, Galway, NY, c. 1860

Humiston & Commings, S. Amboy, NJ, c. 1830–50

Humiston & Stockwell, S. Amboy, NJ, c. 1830–50

Humiston & Warner, S. Amboy, NJ, c. 1830–50

Hummel, J. M., Florence, MO, c. 1860–90

Jennings, Andrew, Galena, IL, c. 1880–87

Johnson, Whitmore & Co., Akron, OH, 1856–62

Jugtown Pottery, Seagrove, NC, 1921–

Kansas City Pottery, Kansas City, MO, 1888–91

Kauffer, H., & Fittler, T., Mankato, MN, c. 1860–78

Kendall, L., Chelsea, MA, 1836–c. 70

Kirkpatrick, C. & W. (Anna Pottery), Anna, IL, 1859–c. 90

Lafever Pottery, Baxter, TN, c. 1840–1900

Lamson & Swasey, Portland, ME, 1875–c. 84

Laufersweiler, F., Manhattan, NY, 1876–89

Lehman & Co., L., Manhattan, NY, 1858–63

Lehman & Riedinger, Poughkeepsie, NY, 1854–57

Lent, B., Caldwell, NJ, c. 1820

Lent, G., Troy, NY, c. 1820–24

Lewis & Gardiner, Huntington, NY, 1827–54

Los Angeles Stoneware Co., Los Angeles, CA, 1900–1903

Louisville Pottery Works, Louisville, NE, 1884–85

Louisville Stoneware Manufacturing Co., Louisville, NE, 1879–83

Lundy & Co., W., Troy, NY, c. 1826

Lyman & Clark, Gardiner, ME, c. 1837–41

Machett, I. V., Barbadoes Neck, NJ, c. 1819–c. 50

Machett, I. V., Cornwall, NY, c. 1859–c. 65

Machett & Son, I. V., Cornwall, NY, c. 1850–c. 59

Macomb Pottery Co., Macomb, IL, c. 1880–1906

MacQuoid & Co., Wm. A. (Pottery Works), Manhattan, NY, 1863–79

Mantell, J., Penn Yan, NY, c. 1855–c. 76

Mantell & Thomas, Penn Yan, NY, c. 1855–c. 76

Mason & Russell, Cortland, NY, 1835–39

Massillon Stoneware Co., Massillon, OH, 1882–1900

Mead, Abraham, Greenwich, CN, c. 1769–91

Mead & Co., I. M., Mogadore, OH, 1840–60

Meader Pottery, Cleveland, GA, c. 1830–1900

Merrill, Earl & Ford, Mogadore, OH, c. 1880–1900

Merrill & Co., E. H., Akron, OH, 1833–1900

Meyer & Sons, W., Atacosa, TX, c. 1887–1940

Minnesota Stoneware Co., Red Wing, MN, 1883–1906

Monmouth Pottery Co., Monmouth, IL, c. 1890–1906

Montague Pottery, Chattanooga, TN, c. 1875–1900

Montell, E. A., Olean, NY, 1870–c. 73

Morable, Pascal, Seagrove, NC, c. 1900–1915

Morgan, D., Manhattan, NY, 1795–1803

Morgan, J., Cheesequake, NJ, c. 1775–c. 85

Morgan & Co., J., South River Bridge, NJ, c. 1805–c. 22

Nash, H., Utica, NY, c. 1837–39

Nash, H. & G., Utica, NY, c. 1832–37

New York Stoneware Co. (Satterlee & Morey), Fort Edward, NY, 1861–85

Nichols & Alford, Burlington, VT, 1854–56

Nichols & Boynton, Burlington, VT, 1856–c. 59

Nichols & Co., Burlington, VT, 1854–60

North Star Stoneware Co., Red Wing, MN, 1892–97

Norton, E., Bennington, VT, 1881–83

Norton, E. & L. P., Bennington, VT, 1861–81

Norton, Edw'd, Bennington, VT, 1886–94

Norton, F., & Hancock, F., Worcester, MA, 1858–65

Norton, J. & E., Bennington, VT, 1850–59

Norton, John, Bennington, VT, 1793–1823

Norton, Julius, Bennington, VT, 1838–44

Norton, Julius, Bennington, VT, 1847–50

Norton, L., Bennington, VT, 1828–33

Norton & Co., E., Bennington, VT, 1883–94

Norton & Co., F. B., Worcester, MA, c. 1865–85

Norton & Co., J., Bennington, VT, 1859–61

Norton & Co., L., Bennington, VT, 1823–28

Norton & Fenton, Bennington, VT, 1844–47

Norton & Son, L., Bennington, VT, 1833–38

Norwich Pottery Works, Norwich, CT, 1881–95

Odum, M. M., & Turnlee, Robert, Knox Hill, FL, 1859–60

Ohr, George, Biloxi, MS, c. 1908–10

Orcutt, Humiston & Co., Troy, NY, c. 1832

Orcutt & Co., Stephen, Whately, MA, c. 1797–1830

Orcutt & Co., Walter, S. Ashfield, MA, 1848–50

Oregon Pottery Co., Portland, OR, 1885–96

Orr & Co., J. W., Michigan Bar, CA, 1859–96

Ottman Bros. & Co., Fort Edward, NY, 1872–c. 92

Pacific Pottery Co., Portland, OR, c. 1892–c. 1950

Parker, Grace, Charlestown, MA, 1742–46

Peoria Pottery Co., Peoria, IL, 1873–1902

Peregrine, P. P., Barbadoes Neck, NJ, c. 1789

Perine, Peter, Jr., Baltimore, MD, c. 1793–1819

Perine & Co., Mauldine, Baltimore, MD, 1827–1938

Perry, S. S., Troy, NY, c. 1827–31

Pewtress, J. B., Perth Amboy, NJ, c. 1840

Pewtress, S. L., New Haven, CT, c. 1868–87

Pharris & Co., C. E., Geddes, NY, c. 1864–c. 67

Phillips, Moro, Camden, NJ, 1867–97

Plaisted, Francis A., Gardiner, ME, c. 1850–74

Porter, Nathan, West Troy, NY, 1846–63

Porter & Fraser, West Troy, NY, 1846–63

Portland Pottery Works, Portland, ME, 1881–90

Portland Stoneware Co., Portland, ME, 1850–

Price, A., Middletown Point, NJ, c. 1847–52

Price, Xerxes (Roundabout Pottery), S. Amboy, NJ, c. 1802–30

Pruden & Co., J. M., Elizabeth, NJ, 1816–79

Purdy, Fitzhugh, Mogadore, OH, c. 1860

Purdy, Gordon B., Mogadore, OH, c. 1865

Purdy, Henry, Mogadore, OH, 1838–c. 50

Purdy, Solomon, Mogadore, OH, 1828–c. 40

Ramsey, B., Halsey, OR, 1864–68

Ramsey, B., Springfield, OR, c. 1853–62

Ramsey, B., & Pollock. W., Albany, OR, c. 1862–64

Ransbottom Brothers Pottery, Roseville, OH, 1900–1908

Ransbottom Brothers Pottery Co., Roseville, OH, 1908–22

Red Wing Potteries Inc., Red Wing, MN, 1930–67

Red Wing Stoneware Co., Red Wing, MN, 1877–94

Red Wing Union Stoneware Co., Red Wing, MN, 1906–30

Remmey, Henry, Manhattan, NY, c. 1789–1800

Remmey, Henry, Philadelphia, PA, c. 1810–

Remmey, John, Manhattan, NY, c. 1735–c. 62

Remmey, John, Jr., Manhattan, NY, c. 1780–92

Remmey, John, III, Manhattan, NY, c. 1791–c. 1831

Rhodes, T., Lincolnton, NC, c. 1865–1900

Riedinger & Caire, Poughkeepsie, NY, 1857–78

Risley, S., Norwich, CT, c. 1846–75

Roberts, W., Binghamton, NY, 1848–88

Roberts & Co., D., Utica, NY, 1827–28

Robinson, Merrill Pottery Co., Akron, OH, 1900–1902

Robinson Clay Product Co. (R.C.P.Co.), Akron, OH, 1902–22

Robinson-Ransbottom Pottery Co. (R.R.P.Co.), Roseville, OH, 1922–

Roche, E. (Hudson River Pottery), Manhattan, NY, 1849–50

Roche & Co. (Hudson River Pottery), Manhattan, NY, 1855–58

Rogers Pottery Co., Thomasville, GA, c. 1830–1900

Roth, Michael, St. Louis, MO, c. 1860–67

Rowley, Wm., Middlebury, OH, 1875–83

Russell, W. D. (Bell City Pottery), Bell City, KY, c. 1890–1922

Ryan Brothers, Ellenville, NY, c. 1875

Sables & Co., T., Medford, MA, 1838–44

Sacramento Pottery, Sacramento, CA, 1855–c. 79

Saenger's Pottery, Elmendorf, TX, c. 1880–1910

Sanborn & Co., John A., Mankato, MN, c. 1880–84

Satterlee & Morey (New York Stoneware Co.), Fort Edward, NY, 1861–85

Sauer, Anton, Louisville, KY, c. 1865–69

Scott & Co., Alexander F., Boston, MA, c. 1870–95

Seaver, J. & W., Jr., Taunton, MA, 1815–c. 30

Seaver, William, Taunton, MA, c. 1790–1815

Selby & Co., E., Hudson, NY, c. 1845–c. 50

Selby & Colson, Poughkeepsie, NY, 1839–41

Selby & Emigh, Poughkeepsie, NY, 1841–44

Selby & Sanderson, Poughkeepsie, NY, 1839–41

Seymour, I., Troy, NY, 1824–50

Seymour, N., Hartford, CT, c. 1790–1842

Seymour, N. & A., Rome, NY, 1815–c. 50

Seymour & Co., I., Troy, NY, c. 1819–24

Seymour & Stedman, Ravenna, OH, c. 1850

Seymour Brothers, Hartford, CT, 1867–c. 71

Shepard, J., Geddes, NY, 1857–c. 64

Sherwood Bros. Co., New Brighton, PA, 1877–1900

Smith, J. C., Mogadore, OH, c. 1860

Smith, W., Manhattan, NY, 1833–61

Smith & Brickner, Albany, NY, 1843–47

Smith & Co., Asa E., Norwalk, CT, c. 1825–87

Smith & Day, Norwalk, CT, 1843–47

Somerset Potters' Works, Somerset, MA, 1847–1909

Somerset Pottery Works, Somerset, NJ, c. 1875

Standish, Alex, & Wright, Franklin, Taunton, MA, c. 1846–55

Star Pottery, Elmerdorf, TX, 1888–1914

Starkey & Howard, Keene, NH, 1871–74

States, A., Greenwich, CT, c. 1750–69

States, A., Jr., Stonington, CT, c. 1778–1826

States & Co., William, Stonington, CT, c. 1810–23

Stedman, Absalom, New Haven, CT, c. 1825–31

Stephens, Truellis, Clyde, KS, 1869–73

Stetzenmeyer, F., & Goetzmann, G., Rochester, NY, 1857–c. 60

Stetzenmeyer & Co., F., Rochester, NY, c. 1853–c. 55

Swan & States, Stonington, CT, c. 1823–35

Swasey & Co., E., Portland, ME, 1890–c. 1930

Swasey, Jones & Co., Portland, ME, 1884–86

Swasey, Lamson & Co., Portland, ME, 1886–c. 90

Symmes & Co., T., Charlestown, MA, 1743–46

Synan, Patrick & William, Somerset, MA, 1893–c. 1913

Thayer, Pliny, Lansingburg, NY, c. 1850–c. 57

Thompson & Tyler, Troy, NY, 1858–59

Troy, N.Y. Pottery, Troy, NY, 1861–85

Tyler, M., Albany, NY, 1834–40, 1843–47

Tyler & Co., Troy, NY, 1859–61

Tyler & Dillon, Albany, NY, 1826–34

Uhl, A. & L., Evansville, IN, c. 1864–87

Underwood, J. A. & C. W., Fort Edward, NY, 1865–67

Underwood & Son, H. J., Calhoun, MO, 1880–91

Union Stoneware Co., Red Wing, MN, 1894–1906

Unser, George, Jeffersonville, KY, c. 1865–69

Van Wickle, N., Herbertsville, NJ, 1823–26

Vaupel, C., Brooklyn, NY, 1878–94

Viall & Markle, Akron, OH, c. 1860–80

Volrath, George & Nicholas, Booneville, MO, c. 1860–70

Wands, I. H., Olean, NY, 1852–70

Warne & Letts, S. Amboy, NJ, c. 1778–1820

Warner, Wm. E., West Troy, NY, 1829–52

Watson & Sanderson, Poughkeepsie, NY, 1839–41

Weeks, F. H., Akron, OH, 1891–1910

Weir Pottery Co., Monmouth, IL, 1899–1906

West Troy Pottery, West Troy, NY, c. 1870–80

Western Pottery Co., Denver, CO, 1906–36

Western Pottery Co., Louisville, NE, 1886–94

Western Stoneware Co., Monmouth, IL, 1906–

Weston, D., Ellenville, NY, 1849–c. 75

Weston, H., Ellenville, NY, 1829–48

Weston, W. W. & D., Ellenville, NY, 1848–49

Weston & Gregg, Ellenville, NY, c. 1869–70

White, Utica, NY, 1838–49

White, N., Utica, NY, 1838–49

White & Co., N., Binghamton, NY, 1865–68

White & Son, N. A., Utica, NY, 1882–86

White & Wood, Binghamton, NY, 1882–88

Whites, Binghamton, NY, 1849–56

Whites, Utica, NY, 1865–77

Whitman, H. M., Havana, NY, c. 1860

Whitmore, Robinson & Co. (W. R. & Co.), Akron, OH, 1862–1900

Whittemore, A. O., Havana, NY, 1869–c. 93

Wilson, Hirum, Guadalupe, TX, c. 1870–84

Wingender, C., Sr. & Jr., Haddonfield, NJ, 1890–1954

Winslow, John T., Portland, ME, c. 1850

Woodruff, M., Cortland, NY, 1849–c. 85

Woodworth, F., Burlington, VT, 1872–c. 85

Wright & Co. (& Son), F. T., Taunton, MA, 1855–68

Zanesville Stoneware Co., Zanesville, OH, 1887–

Zipf, Jacob (Union Pottery), Newark, NJ, 1877–1906

Bibliography

Guilland, Harold F. *Early American Folk Pottery*. Philadelphia, Pa.: Chilton Book Company, 1971.

Ketchum, William C., Jr. *Early Potters and Potteries of New York State*. New York, N.Y.: Funk & Wagnalls, 1970.

——. *The Pottery & Porcelain Collector's Handbook*. New York, N.Y.: Funk & Wagnalls, 1971.

Osgood, Cornelius. *The Jug and Related Stoneware of Bennington*. Rutland, Vt.: Charles E. Tuttle Company, 1971.

Ramsay, John. *American Potters and Pottery*. Boston, Mass.: Hale, Cushman & Flint, 1939.

Spargo, John. *Early American Pottery and China*. Rutland, Vt.: Charles E. Tuttle Company, 1974.

Watkins, Lura Woodside. *Early New England Potters and Their Wares*. Hamden, Conn.: Shoe String Press, 1968.

Webster, Donald Blake. *Decorated Stoneware Pottery of North America*. Rutland, Vt.: Charles E. Tuttle Company, 1971.

Publications

The Antiques Journal
P.O. Box 1046
Dubuque, IA 52001

The Antique Trader Weekly
P.O. Box 1050
Dubuque, IA 52001

Hobbies, the Magazine
for Collectors
1006 S. Michigan Ave.
Chicago, IL 60605

Maine Antique Digest
RFD 3, Box 76A
Waldoboro, ME 04572

Pottery Collectors'
Newsletter
P.O. Box 446
Asheville, NC 28802

Spinning Wheel
American Antiques & Crafts
Society
Fame Ave.
Hanover, PA 17331

Index to Maker's Marks on the Pieces Illustrated

References are to pages on which text descriptions of the photographs may be found.